LAND
Mammals
OF THE
WORLD

BY JUAN CARLOS ALONSO

For Betty and Dalí, your undying
support and endless inspiration make
everything worthwhile.

Love, Juan Carlos

Quarto is the authority on a wide range of topics.
Quarto educates, entertains, and enriches the lives of our readers—
enthusiasts and lovers of hands-on living.
www.quartoknows.com

6 Orchard Road, Suite 100
Lake Forest, CA 92630
quartoknows.com
Visit our blogs at quartoknows.com

Printed in China
1 3 5 7 9 10 8 6 4 2

FSC
www.fsc.org
MIX
Paper from
responsible sources
FSC® C101537

Table of Contents

Introduction

Life on earth is boundless—it is everywhere around us, some of it visible, some of it not. If you were to pick up a handful of soil from your backyard, chances are you would be holding millions, possibly billions, of living organisms.

To better understand the multitude of life on earth, scientists called *taxonomists* have categorized all life into five different kingdoms: *Monera* for single-celled organisms; *Protista* for single-celled organisms with a nucleus; *Fungi* for organisms that absorb the nutrients around them; *Plantae* for organisms that use chlorophyll to absorb sunlight; and *Animalia* for the most complex organisms.

Each and every living thing, right down to the smallest microscopic organism, is classified using the International Code of Zoological Nomenclature, or ICZN. This system divides each organism into seven levels: Kingdom, Phylum, Class, Order, Family, Genus, and finally Species. Some animals are classified as a subspecies, meaning they are very closely related to another species.

We share our planet with a vast number of animal species. A recent study by PLOS Biology estimates there are 7.77 million species of animals on earth. This is in contrast to the 950,000 that have already been discovered and cataloged by scientists. Every year between 15,000 to 18,000 new species of insects, birds, reptiles, fish, and mammals are discovered.

Dog

If we take a pet dog for instance, it would be classified as follows:

Kingdom:	Animalia *meaning it is an animal*
Phylum:	Chordata *referring to the spinal cord or vertebrate*
Class:	Mammalia *meaning it is a mammal*
Order:	Carnivora *meaning it belongs to the group of carnivorous mammals*
Family:	Canidae *meaning it is in the Canine family*
Genus:	Canis *meaning it is a dog*
Species:	lupus *meaning its closest living relative is a wolf*
Subspecies:	familiaris *referring to family or domestication*

Its scientific name is:

Canis lupus familiaris

(Note that the species and subspecies are not capitalized.)

What are Mammals?

Mammals are a class of vertebrate animal (meaning they have backbones) that are defined as being warm-blooded, having hair, and being capable of feeding their young with milk produced from mammary glands. We, as human beings, belong to this class. There are two basic groups of mammals: land mammals (also called terrestrial mammals), the group adapted for life on land; and marine mammals, the group adapted for aquatic life.

Warm-blooded mammals regulate their body temperature by eating food. This allows them to be active even in cold weather, unlike cold-blooded animals that are only active in warm weather. In order to maintain body temperature, mammals must eat more often than cold-blooded animals. Because of this, many mammals spend a great part of their lives hunting, gathering, and eating. Mammals are also known for having large brains compared to their body weight and adapting to a variety of different environments. Mammals exist on every continent and in every ocean of the world.

Mammal Classifications

Because there are so many new discoveries being made, taxonomy is constantly changing. However, there is general consensus in the order classification for mammals (even though several species of mammals are under debate as to where they belong in their class). This book explores 15 orders of land mammals, including:

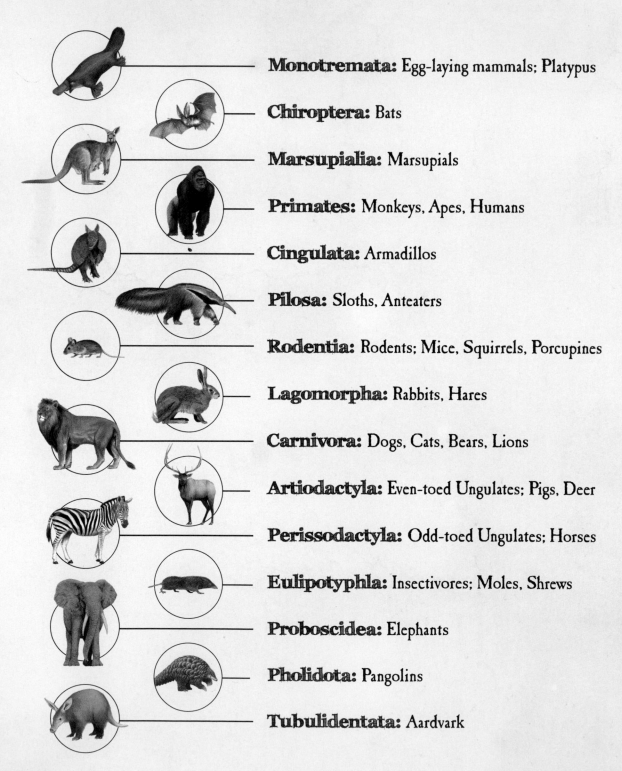

Monotremata: Egg-laying mammals; Platypus

Chiroptera: Bats

Marsupialia: Marsupials

Primates: Monkeys, Apes, Humans

Cingulata: Armadillos

Pilosa: Sloths, Anteaters

Rodentia: Rodents; Mice, Squirrels, Porcupines

Lagomorpha: Rabbits, Hares

Carnivora: Dogs, Cats, Bears, Lions

Artiodactyla: Even-toed Ungulates; Pigs, Deer

Perissodactyla: Odd-toed Ungulates; Horses

Eulipotyphla: Insectivores; Moles, Shrews

Proboscidea: Elephants

Pholidota: Pangolins

Tubulidentata: Aardvark

Within these orders, land mammals have become diverse in their means of locomotion. They have made themselves at home in just about every environment, from arboreal, or tree-dwelling, monkeys to aquatic hippopotamuses to flying bats. Mammals have also adapted specialized features for living in extreme temperatures. In the cold, some mammals have grown thick undercoats of fur or layers of fat to keep warm, and in extreme heat, some have developed a network of blood vessels to regulate their body temperatures. Overall, mammals are a very successful group of animals that have been thriving for millions of years.

In the following pages we will explore each distinct order of land mammal by looking closely at its members, their features, social structures, and unique adaptations for survival on Earth—a planet brimming with life.

Assessing the status of each species

IUCN Global Species Programme has been tracking the conservation status of each species and subspecies around the world for more than 50 years. They have created the *IUCN Red List* to determine the relative risk of extinction. For more information, visit www.iucnredlist.org.

Extinct

Extinct in the wild

Threatened Categories ———— Critically Endangered

Endangered

Vulnerable

Near Threatened

Least Concern

Data Deficient

Each species covered in this book has been assigned a conservation status.

Monotremes (Egg-laying Mammals)

Monotremes are distinctive from all other mammals in that they lay eggs as opposed to giving live birth. Lacking teeth, they have specialized adaptations for feeding. It is believed that monotremes were once widespread throughout the world, but now the only remaining members live in Australia and New Guinea.

Order: Monotremata

Species: 5

Distribution: Australia and New Guinea

Habitat: Platypus is aquatic, living in freshwater; Echidna is terrestrial

Facts: Instead of producing milk through nipples like other mammals, monotremes excrete it through the skin. Monotremes have only one opening in the body to reproduce, lay eggs, and remove waste, called a cloaca.

Dense, waterproof fur around torso, head, and legs

Duck-like bill equipped with over 40,000 sensors, which use electrical signals to find food

Grooved, hardened pads on both the top and bottom of beak to grind food

Larger forefeet with flexible webbing in front of toes that folds back underneath toes when on land

Platypuses

Considered by many to be the strangest of all mammals, platypuses have a duck's bill, an otter's feet, and a beaver's tail; they also lay eggs like a reptile. They primarily live in freshwater lakes, rivers, and lagoons, and hunt shrimp, crayfish, and worms.

Platypus
(Ornithorhynchus anatinus)
Found in Eastern Australia and Tasmania
Length: 12 to 24 inches (30 to 61 centimeters)
Weight: 2 to 4 pounds
Conservation status: Least Concern

Flat, beaver-like tail used as a rudder to steer when swimming and for fat storage

Male platypuses have spurs on their hind feet capable of delivering a powerful venom

Thick spiky fur with spines for protection

Long snout and tongue used to collect ants and termites

Short-beaked Echidna
(Tachyglossus aculeatus)
Found in Australia and New Guinea
Length: 12 to 18 inches (30 to 45 centimeters)
Weight: .5-15 pounds
Conservation status: Least Concern

Echidnas

Also known as spiny anteaters, echidnas look like hedgehogs, though they are not related. They feed exclusively on ants and termites. They use their powerful digging claws to unearth their prey. When threatened, they roll up into a ball. There are only four known species.

Marsupialia (Marsupials)

Marsupials are named for the pouches in which they carry their young. Unlike other mammals, marsupial embryos are not nourished from a placenta. Instead the young are born at an early stage of development and instinctively make their way from the birth canal to the mother's pouch where they can nurse and continue to develop.

Order: Marsupialia

Species: More than 330

Size Range: 2 to 3 inches (5 to 7.6 centimeters), Long-tailed Planigale, to 6 feet (1.8 meters), Red Kangaroo

Weight Range: 4.3 grams (Long-tailed Planigale) to 200 pounds (Red Kangaroo)

Distribution: Australia, New Guinea, North, South, and Central America

Habitat: Forests, arid plains, and trees in most moderate climates

Facts: More than twice as many marsupial species live in Australia than in all of the Americas. With the exception of the numbat, all marsupials are nocturnal.

Large ears

Rectangular head

Red Kangaroo
(Macropus rufus)
Largest of all marsupials
Length: 6 feet (1.8 meters)
Weight: up to 200 pounds
Conservation status: Least Concern

Thick muscular tail used as both a counterbalance for hopping and a third leg when standing

Two fingernails on one digit

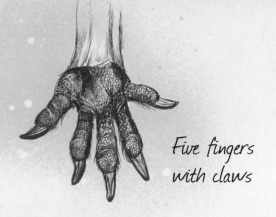

Five fingers
with claws

Long foot about the length of lower leg

Kangaroo Right Foot Detail

Kangaroo Right Hand Detail

Kangaroos

Kangaroos are the only large animal that uses hopping to move around. They are capable of hopping at speeds of up to 35 miles per hour (56.3 kilometers per hour). Kangaroos are mostly herbivores, feeding on leaves, grasses, and occasionally insects.

Bodies covered in short fur

Eastern Grey Kangaroo
(Macropus giganteus)
Most common Australian kangaroo
Length: 5 feet (1.5 meters)
Weight: up to 140 pounds
Conservation status: Least Concern

Baby kangaroos, or joeys, are carried in their mother's pouch for 120 to 450 days after birth

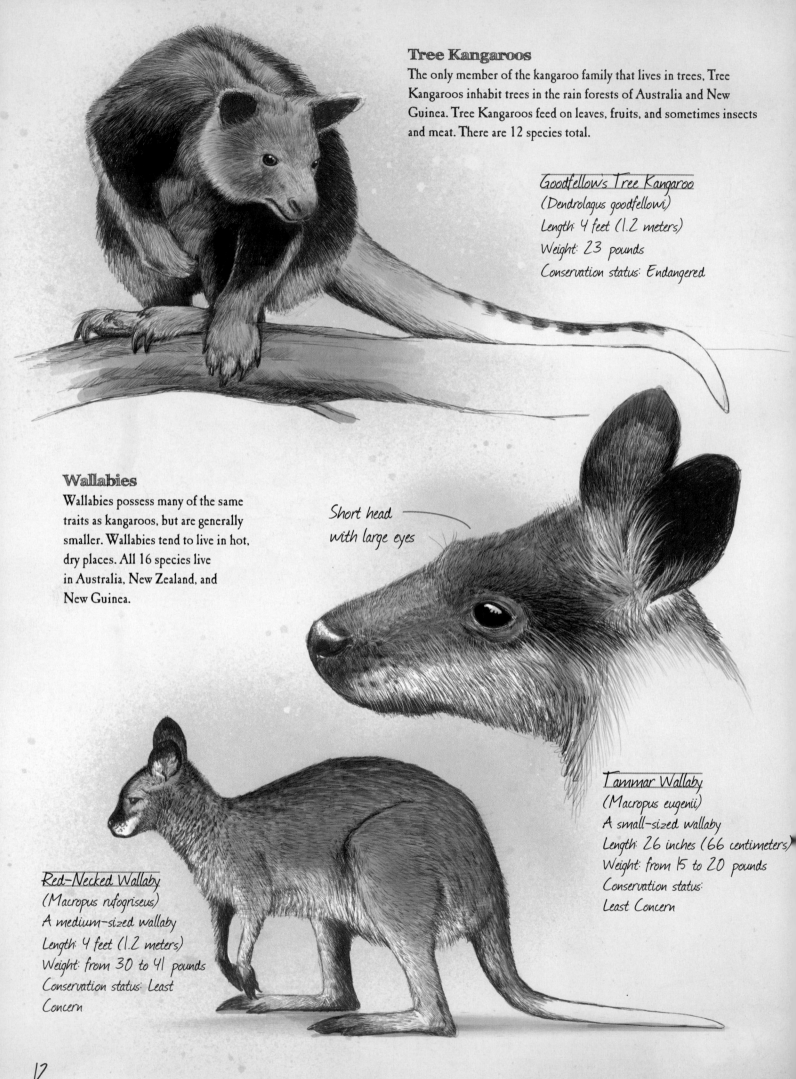

Tree Kangaroos

The only member of the kangaroo family that lives in trees, Tree Kangaroos inhabit trees in the rain forests of Australia and New Guinea. Tree Kangaroos feed on leaves, fruits, and sometimes insects and meat. There are 12 species total.

Goodfellow's Tree Kangaroo
(Dendrolagus goodfellowi)
Length: 4 feet (1.2 meters)
Weight: 23 pounds
Conservation status: Endangered

Wallabies

Wallabies possess many of the same traits as kangaroos, but are generally smaller. Wallabies tend to live in hot, dry places. All 16 species live in Australia, New Zealand, and New Guinea.

Short head with large eyes

Tammar Wallaby
(Macropus eugenii)
A small-sized wallaby
Length: 26 inches (66 centimeters)
Weight: from 15 to 20 pounds
Conservation status: Least Concern

Red-Necked Wallaby
(Macropus rufogriseus)
A medium-sized wallaby
Length: 4 feet (1.2 meters)
Weight: from 30 to 41 pounds
Conservation status: Least Concern

Koalas

Koalas are the last remaining species of the Phascolarctidae family. Unlike the kangaroo, koala pouches open toward the bottom of the animal. Babies are protected from falling out because the pouch remains closed while the baby is inside. They live entirely in trees and feed on eucalyptus leaves.

After 6 months in its mother's pouch, the baby koala, or joey, will ride on its mother until it's one year old.

Koala
(Phascolarctos cinereus)
Found in Eastern Australia
Length: 23 to 33 inches (58 to 84 centimeters)
Weight: 20 pounds
Conservation status: Least Concern

Tasmanian Devils

Tasmanian Devils were given their name because of their ferocity, especially when defending their meal. They are the largest carnivorous marsupials in the world. They feed mostly on birds, snakes, fish, and insects.

Tasmanian Devil
(Sarcophilus harrisii)
Found in Tasmania
Length: 30 inches (76 centimeters)
Weight: 26 pounds
Conservation status: Endangered

Tasmanian Devils have one of the most powerful bites of any mammal for its body weight.

Extra fat stored in tail

Rear legs shorter than front legs

Dark black/brown fur with a white marking on chest

Sugar gliders eat mostly insects and sap from trees.

Sugar Gliders

Living predominantly in trees, sugar gliders effortlessly glide from tree to tree. They are found in Australia, Indonesia, and New Guinea.

Patagium, or membranes, between arms and legs create a gliding wing

Fused second and third digits on feet

Sugar Glider
(Petaurus breviceps)
Length: 12 inches (30 centimeters), including tail
Weight: 4.7 ounces
Conservation status: Least Concern

Wombat

Wombats are relatively large and muscular marsupials from Australia and Tasmania. They are impressive diggers that create elaborate burrows. They use their large and sharp incisor teeth, which resemble those of rodents, to gnaw grasses, herbs, bark, and roots. There are three species of wombats.

Thick coarse fur

Long hairy tail

Short legs

Common Wombat
(Vombatus ursinus)
Length: 40 inches (1 meter); Weight: 57 pounds
Conservation status: Least Concern

Large digging claws

Opossums

Opossums are mostly *arboreal*, or tree-dwelling, and omnivorous, feeding on both meat and plants. They have strong immune systems, making them resistant to many venomous snake bites and diseases. There are more than 100 species total.

Wiry coat of hair

Virginia Opossum

(Didelphis virginiana)
Found in the United States and Mexico
Length: 38 inches (96 centimeters), including tail
Weight: 12 pounds
Conservation status: Least Concern

Prehensile hairless tail

Numbat

Numbats are found only in Western Australia and feed almost exclusively on termites. They are the only marsupial that is diurnal, or active during the day, and are about the size of a house cat.

Numbat

(Myrmecobius fasciatus)
Length: 15 inches (38 centimeters)
Weight: 24 ounces
Conservation status: Endangered

Fur adorned with colorful bands

Long snout and tongue used to collect termites

15

Chiroptera (Bats)

Bats have the distinction of being the only mammal capable of self-sustained flight. They are an extremely diverse group of animals and comprise more than 20 percent of all mammal species. Bats are divided into two main suborders: Megachiroptera, which includes large fruit-eating bats, and Microchiroptera, which includes the smaller insect-eating bats. Though the majority of the species feed on either insects or fruit, some feed on fish or frogs, and three species live entirely on the blood of live animals.

Order: *Chiroptera*

Species: *More than 1,200*

Size Range: *6.7-inch (17-centimeter) wingspan, Bumblebee Bat, to*

6-foot (1.8-meter) wingspan, Giant Golden-crowned Flying Fox

Weight Range: *2 grams (Bumblebee Bat) to*

2.6 lbs (Giant Golden-crowned Flying Fox)

Distribution: *Worldwide, except extremely cold regions*

Habitat: *Caves, trees, and man-made structures*

Facts: *Insect-eating bats can eat their own body weight in*

mosquitoes in one night. Some bats can reach speeds of up to 60 mph.

Bats can live more than 30 years.

Membrane with blood vessels between thin layers of flexible skin and muscle

Some bats navigate and find food by making a chirping or clicking sound. As the sound waves bounce off an object, they create an echo. This echo bounces back to the bat, telling it the distance and size. This is called "echolocation."

Five-fingered hands with four digits fastened together by wing membrane

Large ears to capture the echo signal

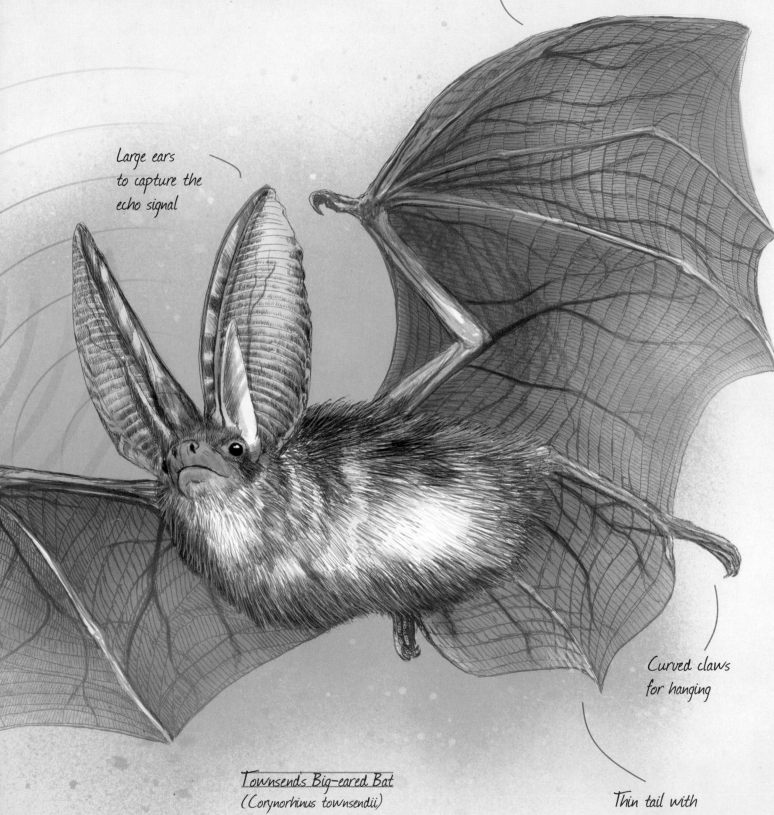

Curved claws for hanging

Townsends Big-eared Bat
(Corynorhinus townsendii)
Found in North America
Wingspan: 13 inches (33 centimeters)
Weight: .5 ounce
Conservation status: Least Concern

Thin tail with membrane attached to legs

Microchiroptera (Microbats)

The microbat suborder includes the smaller species of bats. The majority use echolocation to navigate and hunt insects in midair. Because of this, microbat eyes are smaller than those on megabat species. Microbats are very diverse in appearance due to the adaptations of their ears, noses, and mouths for eating and echolocation.

California Leaf-nosed Bat
(Macrotus californicus)
Found in Mexico and the United States
Wingspan: 13 inches (33 centimeters)
Weight: .45 ounces
Conservation status: Least Concern

Thumb with claw

Large thin-walled ears

Small eyes

Leaf-shaped nose

Base of wing attaches to ankle

Torso covered in think fur

Ears larger
than head
with ridges to
pick up
echo signals

Long appendage
rising from nose
used to assist
in echolocation

Spotted Bat
(Euderma maculatum)
Found in North America
Wingspan: 13 inches (33 centimeters)
Weight: .5 ounce
Conservation status: Least Concern

Tomes's Sword-nosed Bat
(Lonchorhina aurita)
Found in South and Central America
Wingspan: 14 inches (36 centimeters)
Weight: .5 ounce
Conservation status: Least Concern

Head slopes back
with ears directly
at the sides

Notch in lower
lip used to
drink blood

Flattened head with
ears directly above

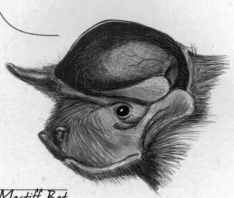

Common Vampire Bat
(Desmodus rotundus)
Found in the Americas
Wingspan: 7 inches (18 centimeters)
Weight: 2 ounces
Conservation status: Least Concern

Western Mastiff Bat
(Eumops perotis)
Found in the Americas
Wingspan: 22 inches (55 centimeters)
Weight: 2.5 ounces
Conservation status: Decreasing

Flattened,
horseshoe-shaped
nose with
elaborate fleshy
growths

Ears pointing
outward from
sides

Short, squared
snout

Decken's Horseshoe Bat
(Rhinolophus deckenii)
Found in Tanzania and Kenya, Africa
Wingspan: 11 inches (28 centimeters)
Weight: .25 ounce
Conservation status: Near Threatened

Big Brown Bat
(Eptesicus fuscus)
Found in the Americas and the Caribbean
Wingspan: 12 inches (30 centimeters)
Weight: .5 ounce
Conservation status: Least Concern

Megachiroptera (Megabats)

As the name implies, megabats are a suborder of bats that includes the largest species. Most megabats have large eyes and smaller ears and feed predominantly on fruit. They use sight and smell to locate food and, with the exception of one species, do not possess echolocation capabilities.

The Giant Golden-crowned Flying Fox has a massive wingspan of 6 feet (1.8 meters)

Unlike microbats, megabats do not have tails

Bats are most comfortable hanging from their feet when not flying.

Bat babies, or pups, hang on their mother and nurse for approximately 3 to 6 weeks. Shortly afterward, they are capable of flying and hunting for their own food.

Straw-colored Fruit Bat
(Eidolon helvum)
Found throughout Africa
Wingspan: 30 inches (76 centimeters)
Weight: 12 ounces
Conservation status: Near Threatened, decreasing

Triangular ears

Long, fox-like snout

Pronounced snout with wrinkles around mouth and nose

Giant Golden-crowned Flying Fox
(Acerodon jubatus)
Found in the Philippines
Wingspan: 6 feet (1.8 meters); Weight: 2.6 pounds
Conservation status: Near Threatened, decreasing

Hammer-Headed Bat
(Hypsignathus monstrosus)
Found in equatorial Africa
Wingspan: 38 inches (97 centimeters)
Weight: 13 ounces
Conservation status: Least Concern

Tubular nostrils projecting from nose

Large rounded lips

Elongated snout with long tongue designed to reach nectar in flowers

Philippine Tube-Nosed Bat
(Nyctimene rabori)
Found in the Philippines
Wingspan: 22 inches (55 centimeters)
Weight: 8 ounces
Conservation status: Endangered

Long-Tongued Nectar Bat
(Macroglossus minimus)
Found in Indonesia
Wingspan: 10 inches (25 centimeters)
Weight: .7 ounces
Conservation status: Least Concern

Rounded head with flat face and short muzzle

White markings on face

Long, squared snout

Fijian Monkey-Faced Bat
(Mirimiri acrodonta)
Found in Fiji
Wingspan: 20 inches (51 centimeters)
Weight: 8 ounces
Conservation status: Critically Endangered

Wallace's Stripe-Faced Fruit Bat
(Styloctenium wallacei)
Found in Macassar, Indonesia
Wingspan: 5 feet (1.5 meters)
Weight: 1.3 pounds
Conservation status: Near Threatened

Primates (Apes, Monkeys & Prosimians)

As part of the animal kingdom, humans *(Homo sapiens)* fall under the order of primates. This order is very diverse and contains many human-like species, including our closest relative, the chimpanzee. The Primate order can be divided into two suborders: Anthropoids and Prosimians. The Anthropoid suborder, being the most diverse of the two, is divided further into two families: Old World Anthropoids and New World Anthropoids. The Old World family contains the great apes, the lesser apes, monkeys found in Africa and Asia, and humans. The New World family includes all species of monkeys found in the Americas. The Prosimian suborder includes lemurs and tarsiers, which mostly inhabit Madagascar, Eastern Africa, and parts of Asia. Primates have a large brain size to body weight ratio, making them smart and successful at adapting to environmental changes. Many are capable of using tools and problem solving.

Order: *Primate*

Species: *Approximately 260*

Size Range: *6 to 9 inches (15 to 22 centimeters), Pygmy Mouse Lemur,*
to 5 feet, 11 inches (1.8 meters), Eastern Gorilla

Weight Range: *1 ounce (Pygmy Mouse Lemur) to 500 pounds (Eastern Gorilla)*

Distribution: *Africa, Asia, and South and Central America*

Habitat: *Primarily tropical rain forests, also mountainous areas*

Facts: *Gorillas and chimpanzees are so genetically similar to humans that many diseases can be transmitted between species. While in captivity, gorillas are given the same vaccines as human babies. More primate species use tools than any other group of animals. Because of their habitat in dense rain forests, many primate species are not accounted for. As many as six new species are discovered annually.*

<u>Common Squirrel Monkey</u>
(Saimiri sciureus)
Found in tropical rain forests in South America
Length: 14 inches (35 centimeters),
head and body
Weight: 2 pounds
Conservation status: Near Threatened,
decreasing

Non-prehensile tail used to aid in balance

Primate Family Tree

Anthropoids

Prosimians
Lemurs, Tarsiers, Lorises

Old World Anthropoids

New World Anthropoids (Monkeys)
Howler, Spider, Squirrel Monkeys

Apes

Old World **Monkeys**
Colobus Monkeys, Mandrills, Baboons

Lesser Apes
Gibbons

Great Apes
Chimpanzees, Gorillas, Orangutans

Round head with white "mask" around face

Squirrel Monkeys live in groups of up to 500 individuals, spending all of their time in trees.

23

Great Apes

Chimpanzees

Chimpanzees are the closest living relative to humans. We share more than 98 percent of our DNA with them. They are very social, living in groups of several dozen to a hundred individuals. Chimpanzees belong to the genus *Pan*, which is divided into two very similar looking species: Bonobos *(Pan paniscus)* are generally smaller and have a female-dominated social structure, while chimpanzees *(Pan troglodytes)* are larger and have a male-dominated social structure. Both eat mostly fruit, but chimpanzees are also known to eat insects, bird eggs, and other primates, including colobus monkeys.

Chimpanzee
(Pan troglodytes)
Found in Western and Central Africa, from tropical climates to more arid savannas
Length: 3 feet, 10 inches (1.2 meters)
Weight: 130 pounds
Conservation status: Endangered

Baby chimpanzees are born with lighter faces that get darker as they mature

Female chimpanzees give birth to a single offspring that they carry until the age of two.

Chimpanzees generally "knuckle walk" when on the ground, but are very good climbers. They spend most of their time in trees.

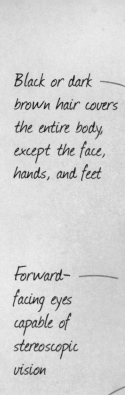

Black or dark brown hair covers the entire body, except the face, hands, and feet

Large ears

Forward-facing eyes capable of stereoscopic vision

Flattened wide nose

Large mouth equipped with large teeth

An adult chimpanzee is a powerful animal—much stronger than a human.

Large toe positioned like an opposable thumb

Human-like hand with opposable thumb and large palm.

Small thumb compared to human hand

Feet adapted for a life in the trees.

Chimpanzee Right Hand Detail

Chimpanzee Right Foot Detail

Gorillas

Gorillas are the largest of all primates and the second closest primate related to humans. They consist of two species: Eastern and Western Gorilla (*G. beringei* and *G. gorilla*, respectively) as well as four subspecies. Unlike chimpanzees, gorillas spend most of their time on the ground and use "knuckle walking" as a main form of locomotion. They are foragers and eat a mostly vegetarian diet consisting of fruits, foliage, plant shoots, and occasionally, insects. Gorillas are found in Africa and, depending on the species, live in either mountainous or swamp forests. The largest gorilla species is the Eastern Lowland Gorilla *(G. beringei graueri)*. Several physical features distinguish male and female gorillas, including size.

Threat display consists of chest pounding, vocalizations and showing its teeth

Females are about half the weight of the males and have a shorter arm span. They also lack the males' head crest.

Large canine teeth

32 teeth (just like humans)

Female's protective posture

A female lowland gorilla nurses its young for the first two to two-and-a-half years of its life.

Eastern Lowland Gorilla
(Gorilla beringei graueri, a subspecies of G. beringei) Found in dense mountainous forests in Central Africa, the Eastern Lowland Gorilla is also known as Grauer's Gorilla.
Height: 5 feet, 10 inches (1.8 meters)
Weight: 500 pounds
Conservation status: Critically Endangered

Males have a large crest with reddish coloring on their head

Deep brow ridge over eyes

Large nostrils

Massive arms with an arm span longer than its height

Mature males develop a gray or silver pattern on their backs, giving them the name "silverback"

Longer arms than legs keep posture angled upward when "knuckle walking"

27

Orangutans

Orangutan comes from the Malay language of Asia meaning "person of the forest." There are two species of Orangutan: Sumatran *(Pongo abelii)* and Bornean *(Pongo pygmaeus)*. The Sumatran Orangutan is the thinner of the two species with a paler and longer red coat of hair and cheek pads extending from the sides of the face. Bornean Orangutans have a coarse darker red coat, larger cheek pads, and large throat pouches. Both species are well adapted to an arboreal life in the trees of swampy and mountainous forests where they feed on a diverse diet of leaves, flowers, fruits, termites, ants, and caterpillars. Like their close cousins the gorillas, there are several differences between male and female orangutans, most notably the cheek pads and body size.

Very long arms used to move through trees and dense forest

No cheek pads and a longer face

Females have a lighter build than males

Bornean Orangutan (female)
(Pongo pygmaeus)
Found in Borneo in forests
Length: 2 feet, 6 inches (76 centimeters), head and body
Weight: 86 pounds
Conservation status: Critically Endangered

Legs used to assist in climbing and feet used to grasp branches

Large cheek pads called flanges help distinguish males from one another and establish hierarchy within groups

Body covered in red hair with a dark face

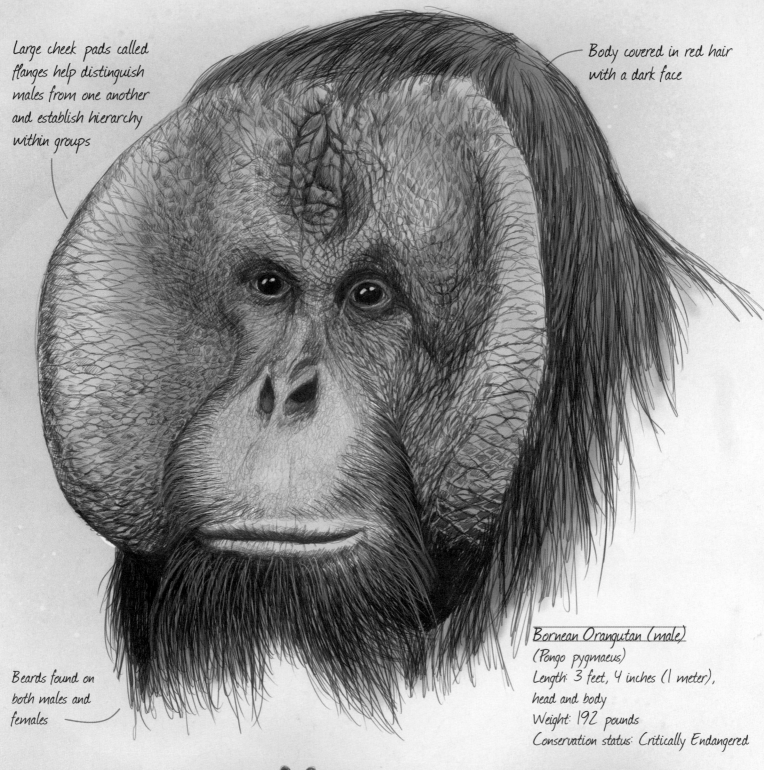

Beards found on both males and females

Bornean Orangutan (male)
(Pongo pygmaeus)
Length: 3 feet, 4 inches (1 meter), head and body
Weight: 192 pounds
Conservation status: Critically Endangered

Orangutans use their hands like hooks to grasp branches with four fingers.

Small thumb size

Orangutan Left Hand Detail

Large toe is used as an opposable thumb to hold onto branches

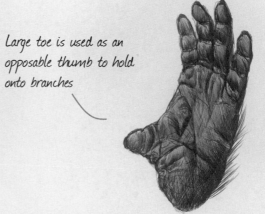

Orangutan Left Foot Detail

White-cheeked Gibbon
(Nomascus leucogenys)
Found in Northern Vietnam and Northern Laos
Length: 2 feet (60 centimeters), head and body
Weight: 13 pounds
Conservation status: Critically Endangered

Male White-cheeked Gibbons develop a tall crest of hair on their heads

Female White-cheeked Gibbon's coat turns from black to golden brown

Male White-cheeked Gibbon's coat is black with white markings on its face, giving it its name

Siamangs have a glossy black coat with a white brow band

Siamang
(Symphalangus syndactylus)
Found in Sumatra, Malaysia, and Thailand
Length: 30 inches (76 centimeters), head and body
Weight: 26 pounds
Conservation status: Critically Endangered

Siamangs are the largest species of the Gibbon family.

Lesser Apes

Gibbons

Lesser Apes (Hylobatidae) are given this name due to their small size as compared to the Great Apes. They include 17 species of gibbons all of which use brachiation, or arm-swinging from branch to branch, as a form of locomotion. Gibbons are capable of moving up to 34 miles per hour through trees, making them the fastest, most agile of all tree-dwelling, non-flying mammals. They can be found throughout Southeast Asia and live in dense tropical and sub-tropical forests. Like many tree-dwelling primates, gibbons feed mostly on fruit, though they also eat leaves, insects, flowers, and bird eggs.

Gibbons have adaptations for living almost exclusively in trees. This includes long arms for swinging, long palms and fingers that are used as hooks, and a wrist joint that is extremely flexible.

Lars Gibbon
(Hylobates lar)
Found in Indonesia, Laos, Malaysia, Myanmar, and Thailand
Length: 18 inches (45 centimeters), head and body
Weight: 15 pounds
Conservation status: Endangered

A white ring of hair around hairless face

Coat color can vary from creamy brown to black. Males and females are generally the same color.

Though arm-swinging is their primary method of locomotion, Gibbons' feet are equally adapted for grasping branches

31

Old World Monkeys

Old World monkeys are a diverse group of monkeys from South and East Asia, Africa, the Middle East, and the Southern tip of Spain. There are 78 different species. They live in several different environments from arid grasslands and tropical forests to snowy mountains. Unlike the New World monkeys, some species of Old World monkeys have adapted to living primarily on the ground. These include baboons and mandrills, which are the largest of all the monkey species. Though almost all Old World monkeys have tails, none are *prehensile*, or capable of grasping. One other feature that distinguishes them from New World monkeys is that their nostrils point down.

Mandrill
(Mandrillus sphinx)
Found in Equatorial Africa in dense rain forests, Mandrills are the largest monkey species.
Length: 36 inches (91 centimeters), head and body
Weight: 86 pounds (females are about half the size of males)
Conservation status: Vulnerable

When threatened, the mandrill will flash its enormous canine teeth as a deterrent.

Thick mane of hair around head and neck

Dominant males develop colorful cheeks to establish their status in the troop

Colorful sitting pads (ischial callosities) on backside

Large cheek pouches used to store food

Macaques

Macaques are the most widespread genus of the Old World monkeys. Their range extends from Japan to the Indian subcontinent to North Africa and Southern Europe, and they are comprised of 23 species. Most macaque species are *frugivorous*, or fruit eaters, while some also eat lizards, leaves, and even human food.

Long-tailed Macaque

(Macaca fascicularis) Also known as the Crab-eating Macaque, they are found in Southeast Asia and are excellent divers. These macaques hunt for crabs in mangrove swamps as well as forage for food.
Length: 24 inches (61 centimeters), head and body
Weight: 18 pounds
Conservation status: Least Concern

Long tail used for balance when jumping in trees

Baboons

The baboon family (Papio) includes five species. They are capable of using over 30 distinct vocalizations to communicate between individuals. They congregate in groups called "troops" that sometimes number over 300.

Brown, hairless sitting pads (ischial callosities)

Males have a mane of wiry hair surrounding their head and shoulders

Olive Baboon

(Papio anubis)
Found in Equatorial Africa, Olive Baboons are omnivores. They eat leaves, insects, bird eggs and other small primates.
Length: 27 inches (69 centimeters), head and body
Weight: 52 pounds
Conservation status: Least Concern

33

Patas Monkeys

There are three subspecies of patas monkey but only one recognized species. Patas monkeys are as comfortable on the ground as they are in trees. They are omnivorous, eating insects, fruits, and leaves, depending on the time of year.

Adult males have a large mustache

Patas Monkey
(Erythrocebus patas)
Found throughout Northern and Equatorial Africa in several different environments, from rain forests to arid plains
Length: 30 inches (76 centimeters), head and body
Weight: 44 pounds
Conservation status: Least Concern

When on the ground, Patas Monkeys walk on the palms of their hands

Mangabeys

Mangabeys are native to Africa. There are 10 species, all of which are highly social. Males are known for making loud vocalizations. Mangabeys feed mostly on seeds and fruits.

Large incisors help with biting through tough fruits

Collared Mangabey
(Cercocebus torquatus)
Also known as the Red-capped Mangabey, they are found in the Eastern coast of Africa.
Length: 26 inches (66 centimeters), head and body
Weight: 22 pounds
Conservation status: Vulnerable

34

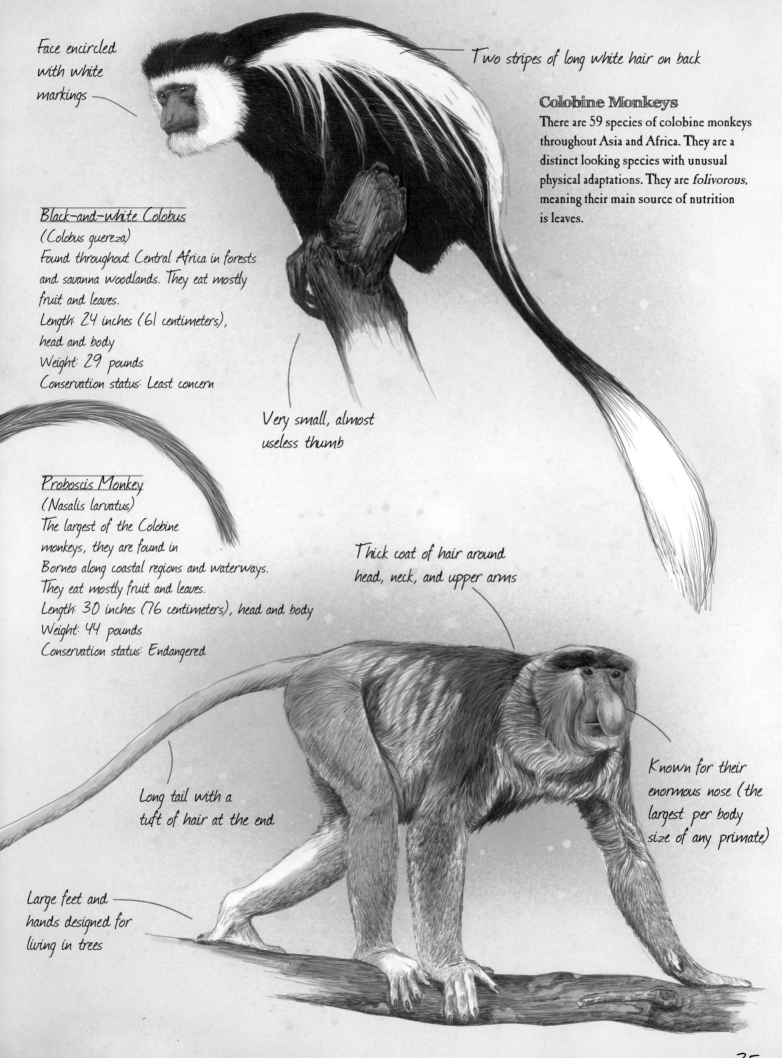

Face encircled
with white
markings

Two stripes of long white hair on back

Colobine Monkeys
There are 59 species of colobine monkeys
throughout Asia and Africa. They are a
distinct looking species with unusual
physical adaptations. They are *folivorous*,
meaning their main source of nutrition
is leaves.

Black-and-white Colobus
(Colobus guereza)
Found throughout Central Africa in forests
and savanna woodlands. They eat mostly
fruit and leaves.
Length: 24 inches (61 centimeters),
head and body
Weight: 29 pounds
Conservation status: Least concern

Very small, almost
useless thumb

Proboscis Monkey
(Nasalis larvatus)
The largest of the Colobine
monkeys, they are found in
Borneo along coastal regions and waterways.
They eat mostly fruit and leaves.
Length: 30 inches (76 centimeters), head and body
Weight: 44 pounds
Conservation status: Endangered

Thick coat of hair around
head, neck, and upper arms

Known for their
enormous nose (the
largest per body
size of any primate)

Long tail with a
tuft of hair at the end

Large feet and
hands designed for
living in trees

35

New World Monkeys

New World monkeys are inhabitants of South and Central America, as well as parts of Southern Mexico. There are a total of 53 species, all of which are tree-dwelling and confined to tropical rain forests. Several species of New World monkeys have developed prehensile tails that are used like a fifth limb to support their weight when in trees. The noses of New World monkeys are flatter, with the nostrils placed at the sides, as opposed to the longer noses with downward facing nostrils of the Old World group. New World monkeys include the smallest species of monkey, the Pygmy Marmoset.

Extremely long and flexible prehensile tail. When not in use, it is held high and curled back.

Long, shiny black coat

Spider Monkeys

Spider monkeys are given their name due to their lanky proportions. Their arms are much longer than their heads and bodies combined. Their tails are prehensile, and are used with the same ease as their other limbs. There are seven species, all of which tend to live in social groups of 15 to 40 individuals.

Black-headed Spider Monkey
(Ateles fusciceps)
Found in Colombia, Nicaragua, and Panama, Black-headed Spider Monkeys mainly eat nuts and fruit, but they also eat insects, leaves, and honey.
Length: 21 inches (53 centimeters), head and body
Weight: 20 pounds
Conservation status: Critically Endangered

Using their hands like hooks to grab onto branches, spider monkeys have evolved without thumbs. They are the only primates to have four-fingered hands.

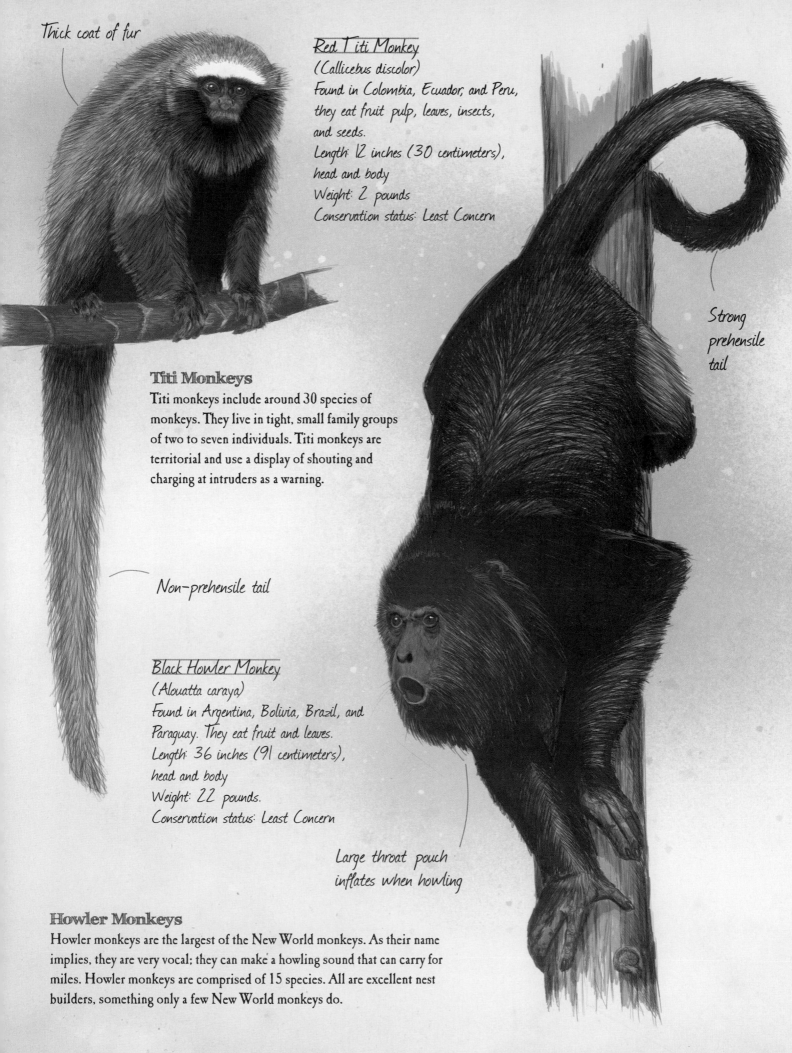

Thick coat of fur

Red Titi Monkey
(*Callicebus discolor*)
Found in Colombia, Ecuador, and Peru,
they eat fruit pulp, leaves, insects,
and seeds.
Length: 12 inches (30 centimeters),
head and body
Weight: 2 pounds
Conservation status: Least Concern

Strong
prehensile
tail

Titi Monkeys
Titi monkeys include around 30 species of
monkeys. They live in tight, small family groups
of two to seven individuals. Titi monkeys are
territorial and use a display of shouting and
charging at intruders as a warning.

Non-prehensile tail

Black Howler Monkey
(*Alouatta caraya*)
Found in Argentina, Bolivia, Brazil, and
Paraguay. They eat fruit and leaves.
Length: 36 inches (91 centimeters),
head and body
Weight: 22 pounds.
Conservation status: Least Concern

Large throat pouch
inflates when howling

Howler Monkeys
Howler monkeys are the largest of the New World monkeys. As their name
implies, they are very vocal; they can make a howling sound that can carry for
miles. Howler monkeys are comprised of 15 species. All are excellent nest
builders, something only a few New World monkeys do.

Large tufts of
hair over ears

Large white mustache

Emperor Tamarin
(Saguinus imperator)
Found in Brazil, Peru, and Bolivia, they
are named for their resemblance
to the German emperor Wilhelm.
Length: 10 inches (25 centimeters),
head and body
Weight: 18 ounces
Conservation status: Least Concern

Common Marmoset
(Callithrix jacchus)
Found in Brazil, they eat tree sap and insects.
Length: 8 inches (20 centimeters), head and body
Weight: 9 ounces

Marmosets and Tamarins
Marmosets and tamarins belong to the family Callitrichidae, which is considered
to be the most primitive family of all the New World monkeys. All have clawed
hands used for climbing instead of grasping hands like most monkeys. There are 22
marmoset species, including the smallest of all monkeys, and 15 tamarin species,
each with unique facial hair displays.

Saki Monkeys
Saki monkeys are
represented by five species.
All of them have a thick
coat of hair, which makes
them look much larger than
they are. They can be found
in Brazil and Venezuela.

Short, coarse
yellow-white fur
around face

Tail covered in
thick dense fur

White-faced Saki
(Pithecia pithecia)
Found in the understory of the canopy in rain forests
where they feed on fruits, seeds, and insects.
Length: 16 inches (41 centimeters), head and body
Weight: 5 pounds
Conservation status: Least Concern

Uakari Monkeys

There are two species of uakari monkeys with four subspecies. All are distinguishable by their short, bushy tail that is usually less than half of its body size. Both species can be found in the Amazon in Brazil, Colombia, Peru, and Venezuela. All are *frugivorous*, or fruit eating.

Bright red head
with no hair

Bald Uakari
(*Cacajao calvus*)
Their head has a bright red appearance due to small blood vessels close to the surface of the skin.
Length: 18 inches (46 centimeters), head and body
Weight: 7 pounds
Conservation status: Vulnerable

Short stub-like
tail covered in
thick fur

Prehensile tail
kept tucked in
when not
in use

Capuchin Monkeys

There are nine species of capuchin monkeys. They are named for their resemblance to Capuchin monks. Their diet ranges from fruits, leaves, seeds, frogs, clams, and even other primates. They are considered to be among the smartest of the New World monkeys.

White-headed Capuchin
(*Cebus capucinus*)
Found across Central America and throughout the Northern coast of South America, they live in groups of up to 40 individuals.
Length: 16 inches (41 centimeters), head and body
Weight: 8 pounds
Conservation status: Least Concern

Relatively large hands used
for climbing

Prosimians

Prosimians are the most primitive group of primates. They are primarily tree dwelling and have elongated snouts with a much more developed sense of smell than monkeys. Prosimians lack the muscles and flexibility in their faces that monkeys use to communicate expression. Many prosimian species use scent to mark territory. They are nocturnal, and have large eyes designed to see in low light and in darkness. Prosimians hunt for small animals including lizards, insects, and small mammals, and are less dependent on fruit than most monkeys. They are the only primates in Madagascar, and are also found in Africa, India, and Southeast Asia.

Lemurs

Collectively, lemurs are represented by about 100 different species. They range in weight, from the 1-ounce Pygmy Mouse Lemur to the 20-pound Indri. Lemurs communicate mostly through vocalizations and scent. All have five-digit hands and feet. An elongated nail or claw on the second digit of their foot is used for grooming.

Tufts of hair around ears make them appear round

Indri
(Indri indri)
Found in Madagascar, Indris have a small head for the size of their bodies and have an upright posture while in trees. They eat young tender leaves, seeds, and fruits.
Length: 26 inches (66 centimeters), head and body
Weight: 21 pounds
Conservation status: Critically Endangered

Very long coat of black and white hair, especially around arms

Hands designed for tree-climbing have a curled appearance when on the ground

Ring-tailed Lemur
(Lemur catta)
Found in Madagascar, Ring-tailed Lemurs spend more time on the ground than most lemur species, but they are primarily tree-dwelling. They are opportunistic feeders and eat everything from fruits to insects to spiders and lizards.
Length: 16 inches (41 centimeters), head and body
Weight: 6 pounds
Conservation status: Near Threatened

The black and white striped tail gives the Ring-tailed Lemur its name

Red Ruffed Lemur
(Varecia rubra)
Found in Madagascar, Red Ruffed Lemurs are known for their very thick red coat of hair. They eat mostly fruit and are fond of figs. Red Ruffed Lemurs live in groups ranging from 2 to 32 and are dominated by a female.
Length: 21 inches (53 centimeters), head and body
Weight: 8 pounds
Conservation status: Critically Endangered

Thick, black fur covers its tail

Torso and legs covered in a dense, short coat of gray fur

Thick, fluffy coat of reddish-brown hair

Black feet and hands

Coat made of two layers: coarse black hair with white tips and a shorter, softer, and lighter undercoat.

Aye-aye

Aye-ayes are a very unique species of primate with their own classification and genera. They are the largest of the nocturnal primates and have one adaptation no other primate has: a unique third finger. This finger is used for tapping and probing to find insects within tree cavities.

Aye-aye
(Daubentonia madagascariensis)
Found in Madagascar
Length: 13 inches (33 centimeters), head and body
Weight: 5 pounds.
Conservation status: Near Threatened

Aye-aye Right Hand Detail

Third finger moves independently from the other fingers and is used for feeding.

Round, flat face with large eyes

Sundra Slow Loris
(Nycticebus coucang)
Found in rain forests in Indonesia and Malaysia
Length: 15 inches (38 centimeters), head and body
Weight: 20 ounces
Conservation status: Vulnerable

Lorises

Lorises are small primates. There are nine species, including the slender and slow loris. Slow lorises are unique in that they have a toxic bite. By licking a secretion from a gland located in their arm, their saliva becomes toxic. They groom themselves and their young with this mixture to protect from attack. Lorises eat insects, fruits, nectars, leaves, and sap from trees.

Tarsiers

There are approximately 10 species of Tarsiers that live in Brunei, Indonesia, Malaysia, and the Philippines in rain forests and mangrove forests. In general, they are among the smallest of the prosimians. They have a unique feature in their spines that allows them to turn their heads almost 180 degrees in both directions. This is helpful because tarsiers can't move their eyes. Tarsiers' hind legs are long and designed to help them leap from tree to tree.

Philippine Tarsier
(*Carlito syrichta*)
Found in the Southeastern Philippines, the Philippine Tarsiers hunt and eat insects almost exclusively. They are capable of producing several different calls which they use to communicate.
Length: 4 inches (10 centimeters), head and body
Weight: 5 ounces
Conservation status: Vulnerable

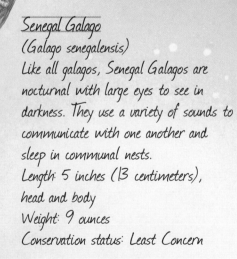

Long, thin hind legs act like a catapult to launch from trees

Mostly hairless tail with feathered tufts at the end

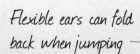

Flexible ears can fold back when jumping

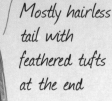

Senegal Galago
(*Galago senegalensis*)
Like all galagos, Senegal Galagos are nocturnal with large eyes to see in darkness. They use a variety of sounds to communicate with one another and sleep in communal nests.
Length: 5 inches (13 centimeters), head and body
Weight: 9 ounces
Conservation status: Least Concern

Galagos

Also known as bush babies, galagos are native to sub-Saharan Africa. There are about 14 species that range in weight from 2.5 to 11 ounces. Galagos are fast and agile; they move through dense woodland forests by leaping from tree to tree. They are capable of jumping 8 to 9 feet (2.4 to 2.7 meters) in a single leap. Their ears are designed to track insects in the air, similar to bats. Their diet primarily consists of insects, frogs, fruits, and tree gum.

Xenarthra (Anteaters, Sloths & Armadillos)

Xenarthra is a superorder of mammals originating from the Americas. It can be broken down into two orders: Pilosa, representing anteaters and sloths, and Cingulata, representing armadillos. Xenarthrans all share a unique feature in their backbones that strengthens their hind legs, allowing them to use their forelimbs for digging or obtaining food.

Order: Xenarthra (includes the orders Pilosa and Cingulata)

Species: 31

Size Range: 4 inches (10 centimeters), Pink Fairy Armadillo, to 6 feet (1.8 meters), Giant Anteater

Weight Range: 4 ounces (Pink Fairy Armadillo) to 90 pounds (Giant Anteater)

Distribution: South, Central, and North America

Habitat: Tropical rain forests to arid deserts

Facts: Members of the Xenarthra superorder have the simplest skulls of all mammals, with peg-like teeth or no teeth at all. Their vena cava, a blood vessel that returns blood to the heart, is made up of two vessels, whereas all other mammals only have only one.

Pilosa

Anteaters

Anteaters are unique because they have specialized skulls and mouths for eating ants and termites. Their tongue can reach lengths longer than their skull. It's lined with tiny hooks called *filiform papillae*. These hooks are used to grab ants and bring them into their mouth where they are swallowed whole. Anteaters are *edentate* animals, meaning they have no teeth. There are four species of anteaters, all found in South America.

Giant Anteater
(Myrmecophaga tridactyla)
Found in Central and South America, Giant Anteaters use their sense of smell to find ant or termite nests. They use their claws to rip the nests open, and use their tongues, which are up to 24 inches (61 centimeters) long, to bring the insects to their mouths.
Length: 6 feet (1.8 meters), from nose to tail
Weight: 90 pounds
Conservation status: Vulnerable, decreasing

Giant Anteaters walk on their knuckles, keeping their long claws from getting worn

Silky Anteater
(Cyclopes didactylus)
Found in Mexico and Central and South America, Silky Anteaters are the smallest of all anteater species. They spend all their time in trees and eat only at night. Silky Anteaters only eat tree-borne ants.
Length: 9 inches (23 centimeters), head and body
Weight: 8 ounces Conservation status: Least Concern

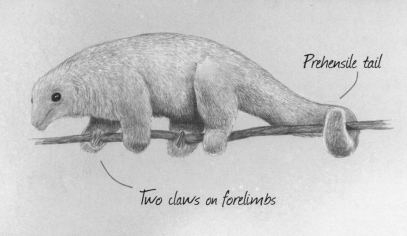

Prehensile tail

Two claws on forelimbs

Long coat of hair with distinct markings on torso

Northern Tamandua
(Tamandua mexicana)
Found in Mexico and Central America., Northern Tamanduas have a prehensile tail used to help them climb trees.
Length: 30 inches (76 centimeters), head and body
Weight: 11 pounds
Conservation status: Least Concern

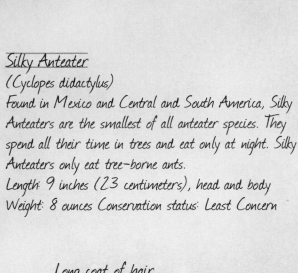

Curved claws used for climbing and opening ant nests

Deep, narrow body covered mostly in long hair to protect from ant bites

Giant Anteaters are nocturnal and, unlike other anteater species, spend all their time on the ground.

45

Sloths

Sloths, named for their slow, sluggish demeanor, spend almost all of their lives in the canopy of rain forests, only coming down to relieve themselves once a week. Sloths have an extremely slow metabolic rate for digesting food, so they move at a slow pace to conserve energy. They sleep an average of 20 hours a day. They eat leaves, tender shoots, and buds from trees. Their food is digested in slow-acting stomachs that are designed to let bacteria break down the plant matter. Sloths spend the majority of their time hanging upside down and as a result, they have developed flexible necks allowing them to turn their head almost 180 degrees. There are six species of sloths, categorized into two groups: three-toed and two-toed.

Two-clawed forelimbs with a hairless palm used for gripping branches

Long limbs with flexible wrists

Hind limbs are as long as forelimbs and have three claws

Hoffmann's Two-toed Sloth
(Choloepus hoffmanni)
Found in Central and South America, these sloths have two toes on their forelimbs that each end in a long curved claw. Though primarily used to climb, they also use them to defend themselves from attack. Hoffmann's Two-toed Sloths have a longer snout than the three-toed group and no tail.
Length: 28 inches (71 centimeters), body
Weight: 19 pounds
Conservation status: Least Concern

Dense, thick fur covering entire body

Brown Throated Three-toed Sloth

(*Bradypus variegatus*)

Found in Central and South America, many can be seen with a green tinge of algae covering their fur. They live a solitary life, except when females give birth to a single offspring, which they carry for about five months.

Length: 30 inches (76 centimeters), body
Weight: 13 pounds
Conservation status: Least Concern

Oval shaped head with small eyes

Black markings around eyes

Mouths curve upward, giving the appearance of smiling

Three toes on all limbs

Longer forelimbs than hind limbs

Short tail

Ears not visible

Algae growth on adults

Cingulata

Armadillos

Armadillos can be easily identified by the leathery hardened shell on their backs. Though their shells can be used for protection against predators, most armadillos use their speed to escape. Only one species, the Three-banded Armadillo, is capable of completely rolling itself into a ball when threatened. All armadillos have large claws on their forelimbs designed for digging and foraging for food. Some live in burrows extending 25 feet deep. They eat mostly insects, grubs, and small invertebrates. Some species have adapted to eating only ants and termites. Armadillos have very poor eyesight and rely on a developed sense of smell to find food. Like many species within the Xenarthra order, armadillos have simple peg-like teeth lining the sides of their jaws. There are 21 species of armadillos, all living within North, Central, and South America.

Pink Fairy Armadillo

(Chlamyphorus truncatus)
Found in Argentina, Pink Fairy Armadillos are the smallest of all armadillo species, and they spend their lives in burrows. They eat mostly ants and larvae, but are also known to eat worms and snails.
Length: 4 inches (10 centimeters), body
Weight: 4 ounces
Conservation status: Data Deficient

Shell only on back

White soft fur covering most of body

Large digging claws

Giant Armadillo

(Priodontes maximus)
Found throughout South America, the Giant Armadillo is the largest of all armadillo species. It uses its enormous front claws to dig burrows and forage for termites, ants, worms, and other invertebrates.
Length: 39 inches (99 centimeters), body
Weight: 72 pounds
Conservation status: Threatened, vulnerable

Hunched posture

Small shell for body size

Long, armored tail

Large muscular limbs with long claws

Southern Three-banded Armadillo

(Tolypeutes matacus)
Found in Argentina, Brazil, Paraguay, and Bolivia,
Southern Three-banded Armadillos eat mostly ants and
termites, but are known to eat fruits and vegetables.
Length: 10 inches (25 centimeters), body
Weight: 3 pounds
Conservation status: Near Threatened

Converts itself into a ball of
armor. Both front and rear
legs and head are completely
protected from attack.

Triangular-shaped
armor on its head
and tail interlock

3 bands

Unprotected underside covered with hair

Nine-banded Armadillo

(Dasypus novemcinctus)
Found in North, Central, and South America, Nine-banded
Armadillos are given their name due to the nine interlocking bands
in their midsection that connect the anterior (front) armor and
posterior (back) armor. Like other armadillos, they use their speed
to evade predators, but they are also known to leap several feet in
the air when threatened. They are generally insectivores, and
are capable of digging burrows deep into the ground.
Length: 20 inches (51 centimeters), body
Weight: 14 pounds
Conservation status: Least Concern

Very long ears

Long tail about the length of body

Four long
claws on
forelimbs

49

Pholidota (Pangolins)

Although they are known as scaly anteaters, pangolins are not related to anteaters. They are the last remaining members of the Pholidota order. Like anteaters, they have long tongues adapted to eat primarily ants and termites. The pangolin's most notable feature is its coat of overlapping scales made of keratin, the same material fingernails are made of. When threatened, a pangolin curls up into a tight ball using its scales as armor to protect it from attack. Its scales are so strong, they have been known to withstand lion attacks.

Order: Pholidota

Species: 8

Size Range: 12 inches (30 centimeters), Long-tailed Pangolin, to 52 inches (1.3 meters), Giant Pangolin

Weight Range: 3.5 pounds (Long-tailed Pangolin) to 73 pounds (Giant Pangolin)

Distribution: Asia and sub-Saharan Africa

Habitat: Burrows and trees in forests, savannas, and grasslands

Facts: The biggest threat to pangolins are humans; they are hunted for their scales, which are believed to have medicinal properties in Asia. The scales of a pangolin make up 20 percent of its weight.

Giant Pangolin
(Smutsia gigantea)
Found in sub-Saharan Africa, the largest of all pangolin species, the Giant Pangolin is terrestrial, living on the ground and spending some of its time on two legs.
Length: 52 inches
(1.3 meters), body
Weight: 73 pounds
Conservation status:
Vulnerable

Large scales overlap to form armor

Long, thick tail with scales extending to the tip

Enormous claws used for unearthing termites and ants

Tubulidentata (Aardvarks)

Although aardvarks resemble a mixture of a pig and an anteater, they aren't related to either. They are the only species belonging to the order Tubulidentata. Aardvarks eat mostly termites and ants, and have thick skin that protects them from ant bites. Like anteaters, they have a long tongue used to lap up small insects. Their large and powerful claws are used to dig deep burrows where they live and raise their young. Aardvarks are nocturnal.

Order: Tubulidentata

Species: 1 (with 17 subspecies)

Distribution: Sub-Saharan Africa

Habitat: Burrows in savannas, grasslands, woodlands, and bushland

Facts: Aardvarks are more closely related to elephants than anteaters. Aardvarks' nostrils can close to keep dust or insects out.

Aardvark
(Orycteropus afer)
Often called "African Ant Bear," aardvarks inhabit about two-thirds of the African continent.
Length: 48 inches (1.2 meters), body
Weight: 150 pounds
Conservation status: Least Concern

Large ears

Body covered in short hair. Some individuals lose hair as they grow older.

Long, thick tail measuring up to 28 inches (71 centimeters) in length

Four triangular digging claws on forelimbs

Carnivora (Feliforms & Caniforms)

The Carnivora order of land mammals is the most diverse order. They range from about 1 ounce to over 1,200 pounds. Carnivora are divided into two suborders: Feliformia for cat-like species and Caniformia for dog-like species. Though Carnivora gets its name from Latin, meaning "flesh-eating," some of its members are *omnivorous*, eating both meat and plants, and others only eat leaves and shoots. All carnivorians share the same arrangement of teeth, which are designed for hunting and eating meat. These teeth include canine teeth for securing prey and the carnassial molars for cutting and tearing flesh. Many popular animals like dogs, cats, bears, and raccoons belong to this order.

Order: Carnivora

Species: More than 280

Size Range: 7 inches (18 centimeters), Least Weasel, to 8 feet (2.4 meters), Kodiak Bear

Weight Range: 1 ounce (Least Weasel) to 1,200 pounds (Kodiak Bear)

Distribution: Worldwide

Habitat: From tropical forests to frozen tundras

Facts: Not all carnivorous mammals are members of the Carnivora order, and not all Carnivora are carnivorous. Animals of the Carnivora order are considered smart and are capable of communicating with each other through either vocalizations, scent marking, posture, or facial expressions.

Carnivora Family Tree

Feliformia (Cat-like)
- Felidae (Cats, Tigers, Lions)
- Viverridae (Civets)
- Eupleridae (Malagasy Carnivores)
- Nandiniidae (African Palm Civet)
- Herpestidae (Mongooses)
- Hyaenidae (Hyenas)

Caniformia (Dog-like)
- Canidae (Dogs, Foxes, Wolves)
- Ailuridae (Red Panda)
- Ursidae (Bears)
- Procyonidae (Raccoons, Coatis)
- Mustelidae (Weasels, Ferrets, Otters)
- Mephitidae (Skunks)

Carnivora are
identified by the
arrangement of
their teeth.

Canine teeth are the
longest teeth. They are
strong, deeply rooted, and
designed specifically for
securing prey.

Carnassial teeth are
comprised of eight large
pre-molar teeth (two on
the upper jaw; two on the
lower jaw on each side of
the mouth). They act as
shears to cut through meat.

Puma
(Puma concolor)
Found throughout the Americas.
Pumas go by many names including
cougar, mountain lion, and panther.
There are a total of six subspecies.
For more information see page 65.

Felidae

Tigers

Tigers *(Panthera tigris)* are the largest in the Felidae family. They can reach 11 feet (3.4 meters) in length and weigh up to 660 pounds. There are six remaining subspecies, all living in Southeast Asia, China, and East Russia. Tigers live solitary lives and are nocturnal hunters. They hunt prey ranging from deer, antelopes, and wild pigs to leopards and crocodiles. By using their muscular frame, they are able to bring down prey much larger than themselves. Tigers are fiercely territorial and are able to defend an area from 30 to 60 square miles (77 to 155 square kilometers) against other tigers or intruders.

Sumatran Tiger
(Panthera tigris sumatrae)
Found in the Indonesian island of Sumatra
within deep forests. They eat macaque monkeys,
porcupines, tapirs, wild pigs, and mouse-deer.
Length: 8.5 feet (2.5 meters), head and body
Weight: 320 pounds
Conservation status: Critically Endangered

Their striped pattern is
unique, like a fingerprint, and
used as camouflage

Long tail, about half of
the body and head length

Hind limbs are longer
than forelimbs and are
used for jumping

Massively built forelimbs
and paws

Small rounded ears

A tiger's eye can see up to six times more than a human eye at night

Large teeth with powerful jaws

Claw in retracted position   Claw in extended position

Front Paw and Claw Detail

Like most cats (Felidae family), the tiger's claws are retracted when not in use. When needed, specialized tendons move the nail out of a sheath and expose the claw.

Lions

Lions *(Panthera leo)* are the second largest of the Felidae family. They are known for their strength and size, earning them the nickname "king of the jungle." They live in social groups called *prides*, which are made up of one or two male lions, four to six females, and their offspring. The females are generally smaller than the males, and lack the bushy mane males are known for. Within the social group, females are responsible for hunting, which is done at night. The males patrol the perimeter of the pride to protect it from intruders. Lions prefer to scavenge for their meals, but they are skilled hunters capable of bringing down large prey using pack-hunting techniques. Their prey consists of wildebeests, zebras, antelopes, wild hogs, buffalos, and giraffes. There are a total of eight subspecies of lions all found in sub-Saharan Africa and in India living in savanna grasslands.

Large eyes with keen eyesight

Females are smaller and have a lighter build than the males

Large muscular limbs with sharp claws

The male's thick mane runs
from the top of the head
to underneath the torso. It
provides protection to its neck
when defending the pride
from other lions.

Southwest African Lion
(Panthera leo bleyenberghi)
Found in Southwestern Africa and the Democratic Republic of the
Congo, the Southwest African Lion, also known as the Katanga
Lion, is the largest of all lion subspecies. The mane on the males
is generally lighter than in other subspecies.
Length: 8 to 10 feet (2.4 to 3 meters), head and body
Weight: 550 pounds
Conservation status: Vulnerable, decreasing

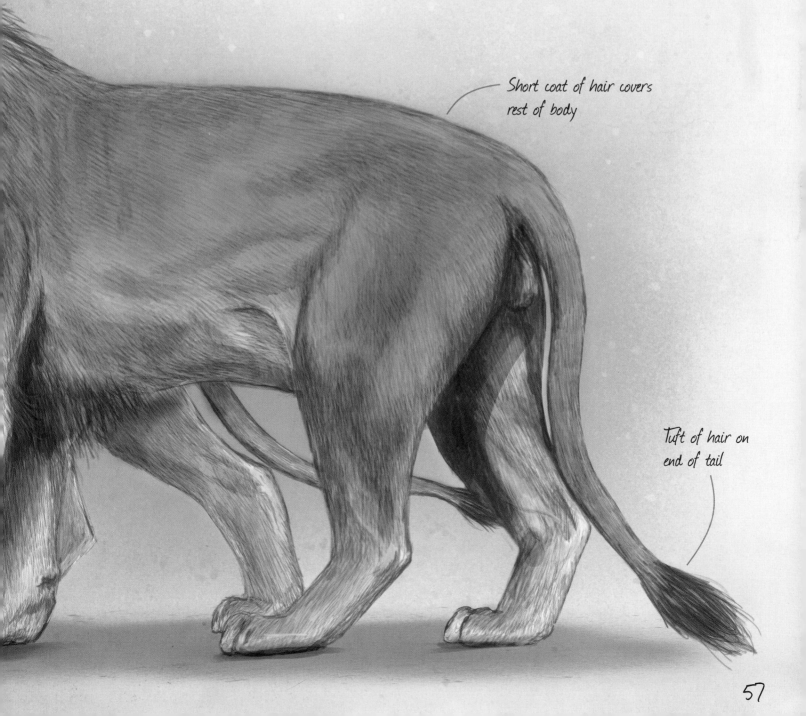

Short coat of hair covers
rest of body

Tuft of hair on
end of tail

Leopards often take their kill to the trees where they can eat without interruption.

A small impala falls prey to a female Leopard.

Ears held back when stalking prey

Long torso

Short legs with wide paws

58

Leopards

Leopards *(Panthera pardus)* are the smallest of the large cats belonging to the *Panthera* genus. There are a total of nine subspecies inhabiting savanna grasslands and dense tropical forests in Africa and Eastern and Southeastern Asia. Leopards are solitary and opportunistic hunters, feeding on everything from rodents and primates to impalas and warthogs.

Once they hunt their food, leopards drag their meal away, often climbing trees to prevent other predators from taking it. The markings on their coat are made up of individual spots called *rosettes*. The rosettes are closely spaced together, forming a camouflage-like pattern, which makes it difficult to be seen when hunting. Leopards are lightly built and very agile. They are able to leap 20 feet (6.1 meters) and run in bursts of 35 miles per hour (56 kilometers per hour).

African Leopard
(Panthera pardus pardus)
Found in rain forests and arid plains in sub-Saharan Africa, African Leopards are diverse in coat coloring, with colors ranging from tan with black spots to completely black.
Length: 3 to 5 feet (.9 to 1.5 meters), head and body
Weight: 60 pounds
Conservation status: Vulnerable, decreasing

Large triangular ears

Forward-facing eyes

Long tail used as counterbalance

Short muzzle with round head

Jaguars are stalk-ambush predators. They use their acute hearing and eyesight to find prey.

An extremely powerful bite force enables jaguars to bite through turtle shells

With a muscular frame, jaguars are very athletic. They are good at climbing and swimming, which gives their prey little chance to escape.

Large paws have five sharp claws on front paws and four on rear paws

Jaguars

Jaguars are the third largest of the Felidae family and the only member of the *Panthera* genus to live in the new world. At first glance, jaguars look almost exactly like their African counterpart, the leopard, but there are several differences. The pattern on jaguars' coats is made up of rosettes like leopards', but the rosettes contain one or two spots within. Jaguars are also stronger and taller than leopards. Their coats vary in color, from all black to dark orange. Because of their size, they are capable of overpowering any prey, making them the apex, or top predator, in their environment. Jaguars feed on over 80 different species, including capybaras, deer, caymans, tapirs, and even anacondas. There are three subspecies of jaguars.

Jaguar
(*Panthera orca*)
Found in Northern Mexico through South America.
Length: 6 feet (1.8 meters), head and body
Weight: 200-300 pounds
Conservation status: Near Threatened

Rosettes with spots inside the pattern

Spots cover almost entire body

Thick, sturdy legs

Black jaguars, also called black panthers, look all black, but they still have spots, visible from close distances.

Cheetahs

Known for being the fastest land animal, it's no surprise that cheetahs *(Acinonyx jubatus)* are built for speed. They have many features that differentiate them from the large cats, including a very slender physique, a long torso with a deep chest, and a small, short face. There are also some physical characteristics that are more similar to canines than felines, like their semi-retractable claws and long flexible spines that give them better traction. Cheetahs reach speeds of up to 70 miles per hour (110 kilometers per hour) in just a few seconds, but can only maintain this speed for up to 1,800 feet (550 meters). These fast, short bursts of speed are used to hunt gazelles, impalas, reedbucks, and springboks. Cheetahs are also known to feed on larger prey such as nyalas, antelopes, steenboks and kudu. There are three species of cheetahs.

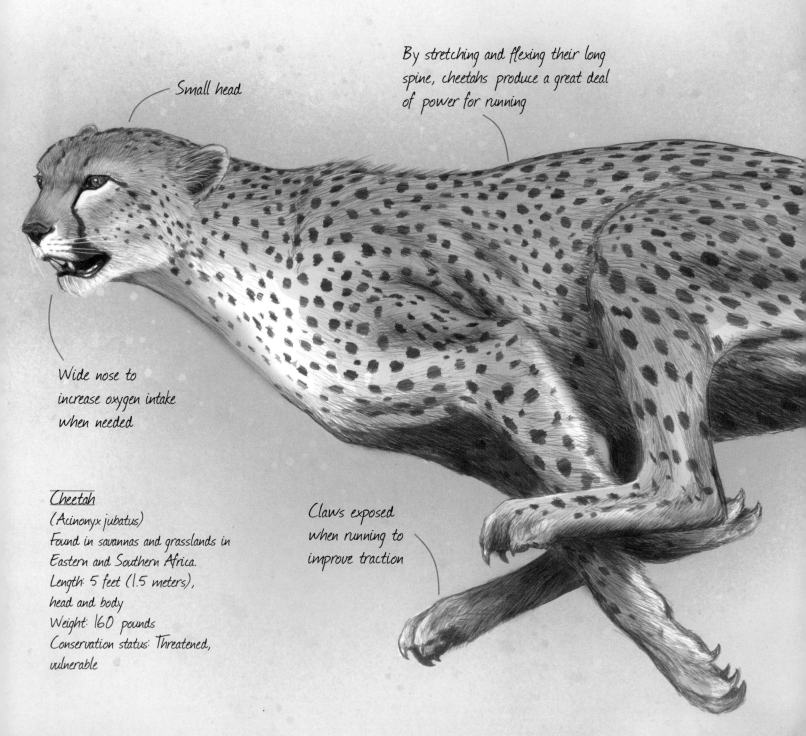

Small head

By stretching and flexing their long
spine, cheetahs produce a great deal
of power for running

Wide nose to
increase oxygen intake
when needed

Cheetah
(Acinonyx jubatus)
Found in savannas and grasslands in
Eastern and Southern Africa.
Length: 5 feet (1.5 meters),
head and body
Weight: 160 pounds
Conservation status: Threatened,
vulnerable

Claws exposed
when running to
improve traction

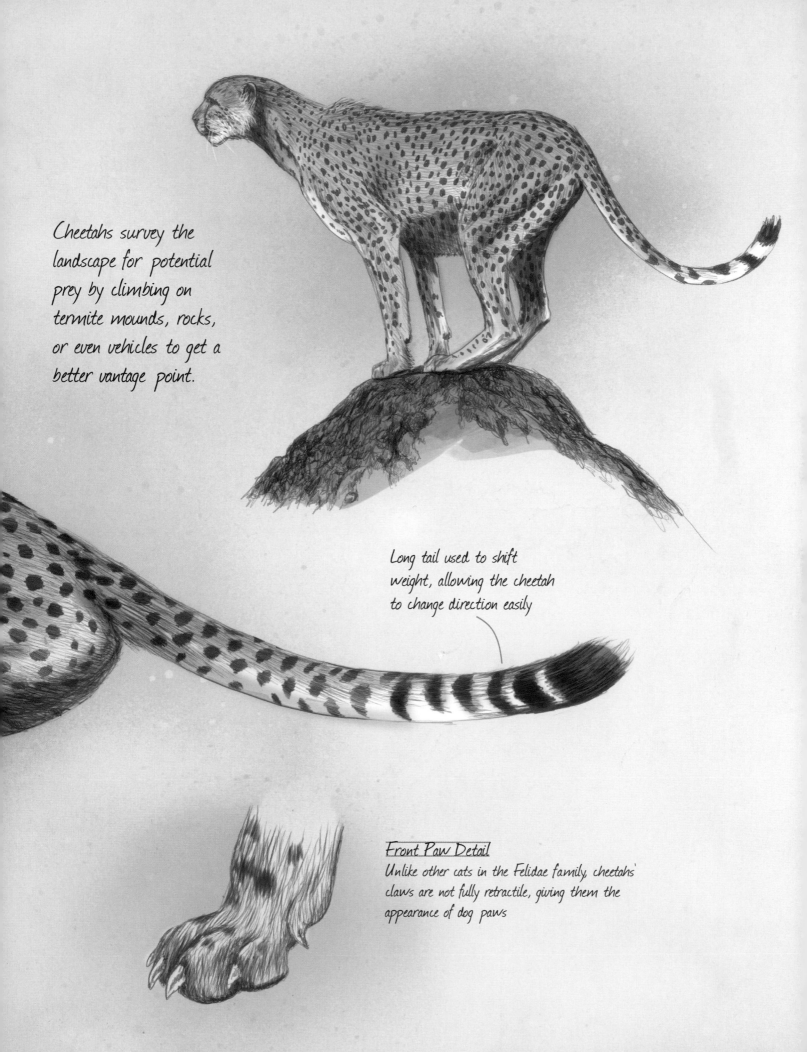

Cheetahs survey the
landscape for potential
prey by climbing on
termite mounds, rocks,
or even vehicles to get a
better vantage point.

Long tail used to shift
weight, allowing the cheetah
to change direction easily

Front Paw Detail
Unlike other cats in the Felidae family, cheetahs'
claws are not fully retractile, giving them the
appearance of dog paws

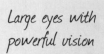
Large eyes with
powerful vision

Snow Leopards

Shorter than most big cats, *Snow Leopards*
(Panthera uncia) are covered in a dense coat
protecting them from cold conditions. Fierce
predators, Snow Leopards can hunt and bring
down prey much larger than themselves,
including camels and Siberian ibex.

Snow Leopard

(Panthera uncia)
*Found in the mountain areas of Central and
Southern Asia.*
Length: 50 inches (1.2 meters), head and body
Weight: 120 pounds
Conservation status: Endangered

Short, stocky legs

Clouded Leopards

Clouded Leopards are medium-sized cats adapted for cold
weather. They are excellent climbers and hunt hogs, deer,
slow lorises, and brush-tailed porcupines.

Clouded Leopard

(Neofelis nebulosa)
Found in the foothills of the Himalayas in Southeast Asia into China.
Length: 43 inches (1 meter), head and body
Weight: 50 pounds
Conservation status: Vulnerable

Very long tail used for
balance when jumping
or running

Dense coat marked with spots, making rosettes with darker coloration between spots

Short coat, yellow-brown to tan in color

Long, thick tail about the length of its body

Large ears

Pumas

Pumas are also known as cougars, mountain lions, and panthers. There are six subspecies distinguishable only by size. Pumas are primarily ambush hunters and feed on a wide variety of species from deer to hogs and even horses.

Coat has a combination of spots and stripes forming a unique camouflage pattern

Puma
(Puma concolor)
Found throughout the Americas.
Length: 4 to 6 feet (1.2 to 1.8 meters), head and body
Weight: from 70 to 200 pounds
Conservation status: ranges from Critically Endangered for the Florida Panther, to Least Concern for the North American Cougar

Wide paws used for climbing and traveling through snow

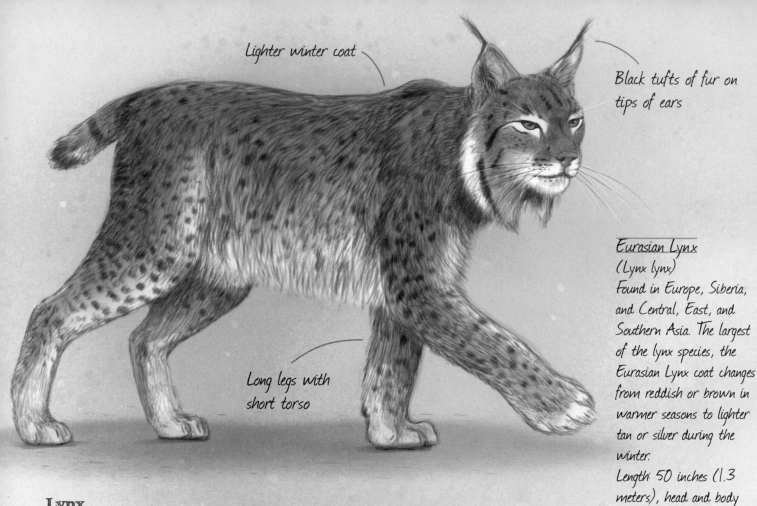

Lighter winter coat

Black tufts of fur on tips of ears

Eurasian Lynx
(Lynx lynx)
Found in Europe, Siberia, and Central, East, and Southern Asia. The largest of the lynx species, the Eurasian Lynx coat changes from reddish or brown in warmer seasons to lighter tan or silver during the winter.
Length: 50 inches (1.3 meters), head and body
Weight: 66 pounds
Conservation status: Least Concern

Long legs with short torso

Lynx

Lynx are medium-sized wild cats. There are four different species, including the bobcat, Eurasian, Canada, and Iberian lynx. Like other cats, they are good hunters, feeding on a broad variety of prey including deer, rabbits, fish, foxes, sheep, and turkeys.

Long torso covered in short hair

Long tail about the length of torso

Short legs

Jaguarundis

Jaguarundis are small cats with small heads, short legs, and elongated torsos and tails. They spend time in trees, but are more commonly seen on the ground where they hunt rabbits, rodents, birds, fish, and marmoset monkeys.

Jaguarundi
(Puma yagouaroundi)
Found throughout Northern Mexico and Central and South America
Length: 30 inches (76 centimeters), head and body
Weight: 20 pounds
Conservation status: Least Concern

Ocelot

Ocelots are medium-sized wild cats with dotted and striped patterns extending from their head to their tails. They are nocturnal and hunt armadillos, opossums, rabbits, rodents, small birds, and fish.

Ocelot
(Leopardus pardalis)
Found in tropical dense forests in Northern Mexico and throughout Central and South America.
Length: 39 inches (1 meter), head and body
Weight: 35 pounds
Conservation status: Least Concern

Large eyes for
nocturnal hunting

Short powerful legs with
small paws

Small head
with short snout

Servals

Servals are a medium-sized cat with a small head, very large ears, and long legs. They are primarily terrestrial, and they hunt small birds, frogs, insects, and reptiles.

Serval
(Leptailurus serval)
Found in wetlands and savannas from Central to Southern Africa.
Length: 39 inches (1 meter), head and body
Weight: 39 pounds
Conservation status: Least Concern

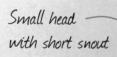

Long slender legs

Viverridae

Civets, Genets, Linsangs

The Viverridae family includes 38 species of small- to medium-sized mammals that inhabit Southern Europe, Africa, and Asia. They are the most primitive of the Feliformia suborder of Carnivora, and all have long bodies with relatively short legs. Viverridae are known for their powerful scent glands that, in some species, are used as a defensive weapon against predators. Ranging in size from the 13-inch (33-centimeter) African Linsang, to the 33-inch (84-centimeter) African Civet, Viverridae are found in savannas, woodland forests, and mountainous regions.

Coat is covered with spots and stripes

Thick, tall mane found on males

Small paws with five toes on forelimbs, four on hind limbs

Head and face resemble raccoon

African Civet
(Civettictis civetta)
Found near rivers and woodlands in sub-Saharan Africa. The largest of all Viverridae species, African Civets are omnivores, feeding on small invertebrates, eggs, carrion, and fruits.
Length: 33 inches (84 centimeters), head and body
Weight: 44 pounds
Conservation status: Least Concern

Long, furry tail about the length of body

Cat-like paws with semi-retractable claws

Common Genet
(Genetta genetta)
Found in Africa and Southern Europe. Common Genets are slender and cat-like with a pointed muzzle. They are nocturnal and solitary hunters. They eat fish, insects, birds, and amphibians as well as fruits and figs.
Length: 22 inches (56 centimeters), head and body
Weight: 4 to 5 pounds
Conservation status: Least Concern

Tufts of hair
over ears

Dense, black coat
protects skin
from getting wet

Binturong
(Arctictis binturong)
Found in Southern and Southeast Asia,
Binturongs are also called bearcats for
their appearance, though they are not
related to either. Mostly active at night,
Binturongs live in trees and eat small
reptiles, small mammals, and fruit.
Length: 30 inches (76 centimeters),
head and body
Weight: 24 to 50 pounds
Conservation status: Vulnerable

Clawed paws with
pads for climbing

Prehensile tail as long
as head and body

Spotted Linsang
(Prionodon pardicolor)
Found in Southeast Asia, from India to Vietnam. Spotted
Linsangs are thin and long with short legs. They live almost
exclusively in trees, and prey predominantly on small vertebrates
such as birds, rodents, frogs, and snakes.
Length: 15 inches (38 centimeters), head and body
Weight: 1 pound
Conservation status: Least Concern

Gripping pad at
end of tail

Long neck

Tail longer
than body

Long, pointed
snout

Low center of gravity

69

Hyaenidae

Hyenas

Though they are part of the Feliformia (or cat-like) suborder of Carnivora, hyenas have many features in common with dogs. Hyenas and dogs both have padded paws with non-retractable claws, they are both completely terrestrial, and they both catch prey with their mouths instead of claws. Comprised of only four species found mostly in Africa and Asia, hyenas are associated with being opportunistic scavengers, but some species are skilled hunters that kill up to 95 percent of their meals. With the exception of the Aardwolf, hyenas have massively built pre-molar teeth designed to break through bone, which they can fully digest. They range in size from 31 inches (79 centimeters) to 5 feet (1.5 meters) in length, and are also known for their laugh-like vocalizations.

Thick, muscular neck

Back slopes downward

Short, rounded, dog-like head

Large, bone-crushing teeth with powerful jaws

Forelimbs much longer than hind limbs

Dog-like paws with four toes

Spotted Hyena
(Crocuta crocuta)
Found in Southern Africa, and the largest of the hyena species, Spotted Hyenas (also known as Laughing Hyenas), are skilled pack hunters and are very social. They can fiercely defend meals as well as steal another predator's meal. Spotted Hyenas hunt mostly gazelles, wildebeests, and zebras by separating the young or weak animals from the herd.
Length: 50 inches (1.3 meters), head and body
Weight: 120 pounds
Conservation status: Least Concern

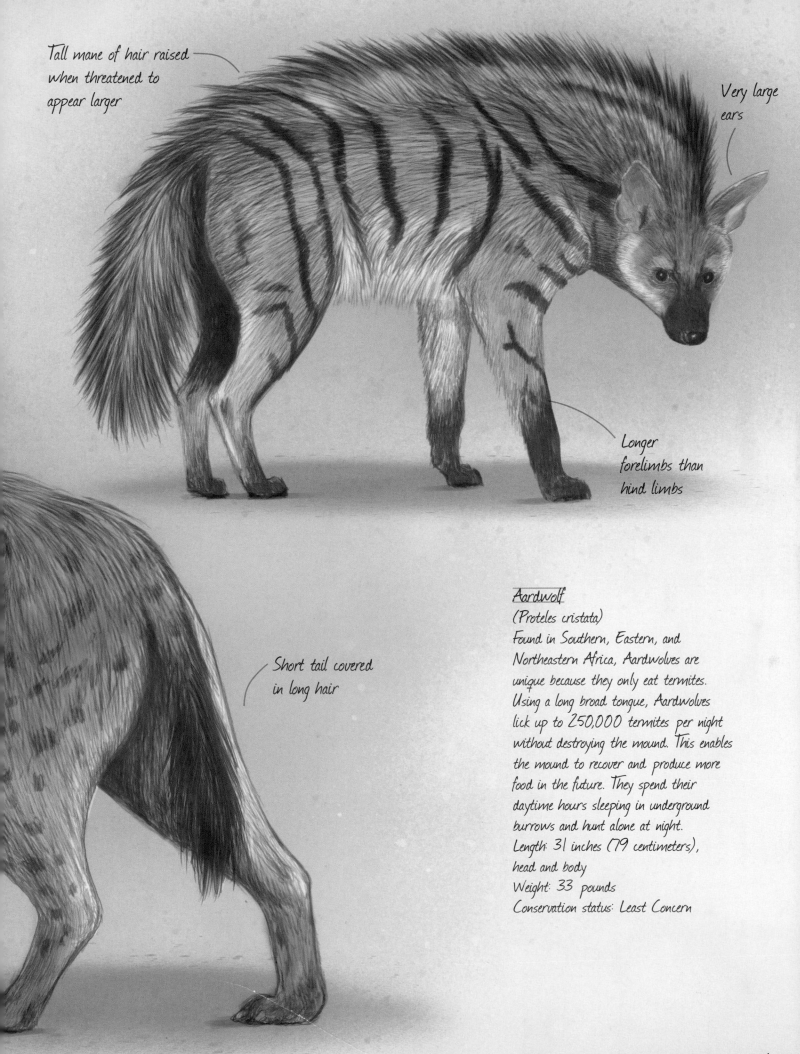

Tall mane of hair raised
when threatened to
appear larger

Very large
ears

Longer
forelimbs than
hind limbs

Short tail covered
in long hair

Aardwolf
(Proteles cristata)
Found in Southern, Eastern, and
Northeastern Africa, Aardwolves are
unique because they only eat termites.
Using a long broad tongue, Aardwolves
lick up to 250,000 termites per night
without destroying the mound. This enables
the mound to recover and produce more
food in the future. They spend their
daytime hours sleeping in underground
burrows and hunt alone at night.
Length: 31 inches (79 centimeters),
head and body
Weight: 33 pounds
Conservation status: Least Concern

Herpestidae

Mongooses and Meerkats

Mongooses are small cat-like mammals from the Feliformia suborder consisting of 34 species. Although originally from Asia, Africa, and Southern Europe, they have flourished in Hawaii, Fiji, and the Caribbean since being introduced to control rat populations. They feed mostly on insects, crabs, birds, lizards, and rodents. Some species, like the Indian Grey Mongoose, are known to kill and eat large venomous snakes such as the king cobra. The Herpestidae family ranges in size from the Common Dwarf Mongoose at 9 inches (23 centimeters) in length, to the White-tailed Mongoose at 28 inches (71 centimeters).

Pointed, triangular shaped head

Like most Mongooses, the Yellow Mongoose has horizontally slit pupils

Large, flat rounded ears

Yellow Mongoose
(Cynictis penicillata)
Found in Southern Africa. Also known as the Red Meerkat, the Yellow Mongoose hunts and eats small mammals, lizards, snakes, eggs and crabs. They are active during the day and live in elaborate burrows with many entrances.
Length: 20 inches (51 centimeters), head and body
Weight: 1 pound
Conservation status: Least Concern

Indian Grey Mongoose
(Herpestes edwardsii)
Found in Southeast Asia, Indian Grey Mongooses are known for eating snakes, most notably cobras. They release a chemical in their nerve cells that makes them immune to snake venom. Along with snakes, Indian Grey Mongooses feed on rats, eggs, and scorpions.
Length: 17 inches (43 centimeters), head and body
Weight: 4 pounds
Conservation status: Least Concern

Long gray coat of thick hair

Long torso

Long claws for digging

Meerkats

Meerkats are highly social animals. They live in groups called "mobs," which contain 20 to 50 individuals. These mobs are organized; sentinels will stand guard while other members feed. Meerkats burrow into the ground to form vast networks of tunnels in which they spend most of their time. During daylight hours, meerkats forage for food, such as snakes, insects, eggs, small mammals, plants, and fungi.

Meerkat
(Suricata suricatta)
Found in Southern Africa.
Length: 18 inches (46 centimeters),
head and body
Weight: 4 pounds
Conservation status: Least Concern

A Meerkat sentinel stands upright on the lookout for predators.

Forward facing eyes with dark areas around them

Coat of medium-length hair with stripes on back side of torso

Sharp pointed snout with rounded ears

Like all Mongooses, Meerkats have an elongated torso.

Five fingers on hands and four toes on feet

Thin tail

73

Canidae

Gray Wolves

Gray wolves *(Canis lupus)*, also known as timber wolves, are the largest of the Canidae family. They range throughout the northern hemisphere in both the Old and New World. They are highly sociable, living in packs consisting of a mating pair and their offspring. These packs can expand to as large as 30 individuals once the offspring reach adulthood. They will then break off into smaller groups, forming new packs. Wolves have many means of communicating with one another, including howling, facial expressions, and scent marking, each used for distinct purposes. There are many subspecies of gray wolves divided into two groups: Old World gray wolves and New World gray wolves. All breeds of domesticated dog *(Canis lupus familiaris)* are close relatives of the gray wolf. They are considered a subspecies, and share many of their traits and innate behaviors.

Eurasian Wolf
(Canis lupus lupus)
Found throughout Europe and Asia, the Eurasian Wolf, also known as the Common Wolf, is the largest of the Old World wolves. They hunt deer, moose, wild goats, and wild boars. Because of human expansion into wolf habitats, many packs prey on livestock and scavenge garbage
Length: 50 inches (1.3 meters), head and body
Weight: 100 pounds
Conservation status: Least Concern

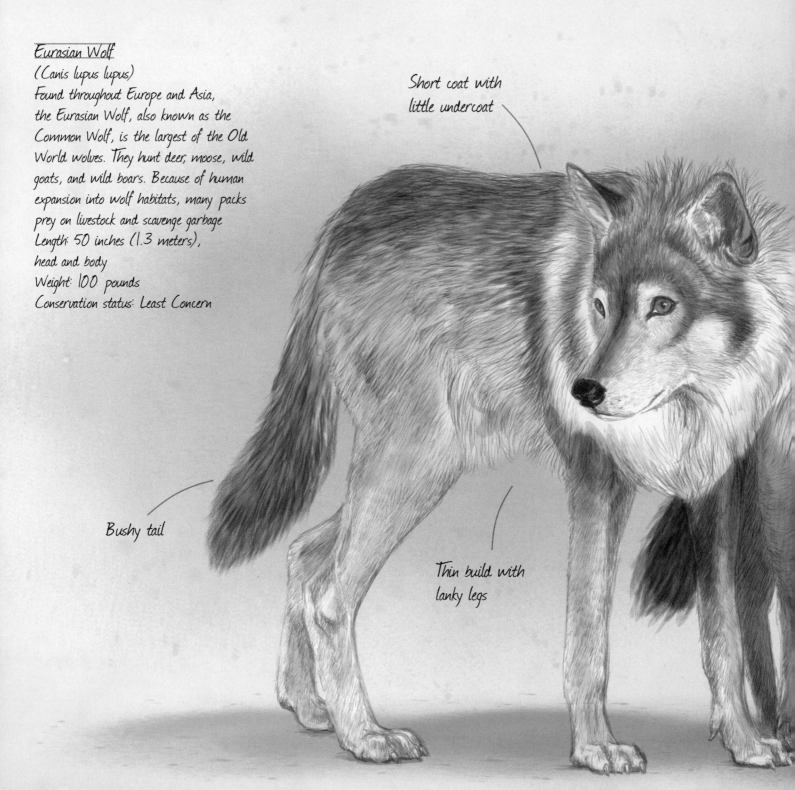

Short coat with little undercoat

Bushy tail

Thin build with lanky legs

Wolves mostly howl to assemble the pack, and to let others know where they are. This cry is often made by a member before a hunt or if separated from the pack. The sound can carry for many miles.

Winter coat of the Yukon Wolf is thicker with a dense undercoat

Robust build

Summer coat has thinner undercoat and is lighter

Yukon Wolf
(Canis lupus pambasileus)
Found in the Alaskan interior and Yukon area. The Yukon Wolf, also known as the Interior Alaskan Wolf, is one of the largest of all gray wolf subspecies. They mostly hunt moose, caribou, and sheep.
Length: 55 to 60 inches (1.4 to 1.5 meters), head and body
Weight: up to 120 pounds
Conservation status: Least Concern

Large paws for walking in snowy conditions

75

Jackals

Jackals are medium-sized canine found in Southeastern Europe, the Middle East, Asia, and South and Central Africa. There are three species: Side-striped Jackal, Golden Jackal, and Black-backed Jackal, all of which live in pairs or are solitary.

Gray and black markings with horizontal stripes

Thinly built head with small eyes

Short legs

Large ears for size

Medium-length coat

Long, thin legs

Coyote
(Canis latrans)
Found in Central and North America. Unlike wolves, some coyotes live solitary lives. Coyotes' diets are varied and include deer, sheep, rabbits, rodents, insects, and small reptiles. They are rarely seen hunting in packs. They are extremely vocal with high-pitched howls and yelps that can be heard for miles.
Length: 48 inches (1.3 meters), head and body
Weight: 44 pounds
Conservation status: Least Concern

76

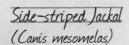

Side-striped Jackal
(Canis mesomelas)

Found in Central and Southern Africa, Side-striped Jackals are the least aggressive of the jackal species. Extremely adaptable to food sources, Side-striped Jackals are opportunistic omnivores that feed on everything from small mammals to invertebrates. They often scavenge other predators' meals.

Length: 32 inches (81 centimeters), head and body
Weight: 31 pounds
Conservation status: Least Concern

Large ears

Reddish-brown coat

Narrow, pointed snout

Maned Wolf
(Chrysocyon brachyurus)

Found in South America, Maned Wolves are the largest South American Canidae with exceptionally long legs used to help them navigate tall grassy areas. They are solitary, nocturnal hunters. They eat mostly rodents, rabbits, birds, and fish, but are also known to eat fruits and tubers.

Length: 39 inches (1 meter), head and body
Weight: 51 pounds
Conservation status: Near Threatened

Legs among the longest per body size in the Canidae family

Tail ends in white tip

77

African Wild Dog
(*Lycaon pictus*)
Found in sub-Saharan Africa, African Wild
Dogs are highly social, living and hunting in tight
packs consisting of 2 to 27 members. Their
coats are made up of stiff bristle-like hairs
with no underfur. They are skilled pack hunters;
they prey on medium-sized antelope, wild
boars, and small mammals.
Length: 40 inches (1 meter), head and body
Weight: 55 pounds
Conservation status: Endangered

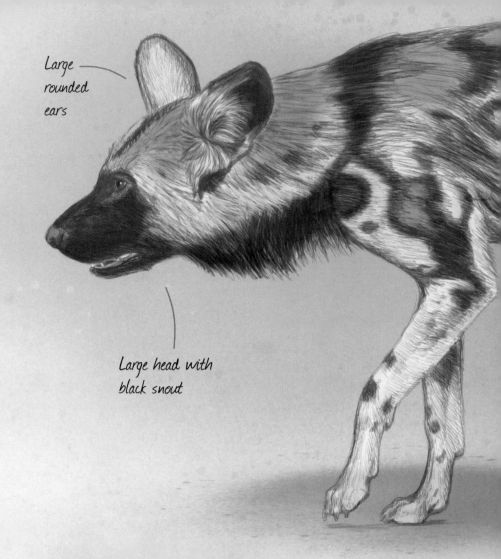

Large
rounded
ears

Large head with
black snout

Foxes
Foxes are small to medium-sized canines found on every continent except for Antarctica.
There are a total of 12 distinct species all within the *Vulpes* genus, ranging in size from the
Fennec Fox (3 pounds) to the Red Fox (19 pounds). Like other canines, foxes are vocal
using sounds to communicate. Most fox species live in small packs, with the exception of
the Arctic Fox, which lives alone.

Triangular
ears

Red Fox
(*Vulpes vulpes*)
Found across the entire Northern
Hemisphere from the Arctic Circle
to North Africa, North and Central
America, and Asia. The largest of the
fox species, the Red Fox has varied coat
colors, from its namesake red to silver
to amber. They primarily feed on small
rodents and mammals but also eat
birds, berries, and fruits.
Length: 35 inches (.9 meters),
head and body
Weight: 19 pounds
Conservation status: Least Concern

Long,
bushy tail

Pointed
snout

Long legs with
black paws

78

Splotches of tan, brown, black, and white give the African Wild Dog's coat a "painted" appearance

Hairy tail ending in a white tip

Thick, furry tail

Enormous ears larger than head

Fennec Fox
(Vulpes zerda)
Found in Northern Africa, Fennec Foxes are adapted for life in the desert. Their most notable feature, the large ears, are designed to both keep them cool, and aid in hearing prey hiding underground. They are the smallest of the fox species.
Length: 10 inches (25 centimeters), head and body; Weight: 3 pounds
Conservation status: Least Concern

Large paws for digging

Light coloring helps camouflage in the snow

Two layers of thick dense coat

Arctic Fox
(Vulpes lagopus)
Found in the Arctic regions of the Northern Hemisphere. With a thick coat and undercoat, Arctic Foxes can survive in the most frigid weather. They prey on small rodents and scavenge carcasses.
Length: 22 inches (56 centimeters), head and body
Weight: 10 pounds
Conservation status: Least Concern

Short stocky legs

Ursidae

Brown Bears

The brown bear *(Ursus arctos)* is the largest of all the land-dwelling carnivorians, with the polar bear (considered a marine mammal) a close second. Brown bears are found across the Northern Hemisphere from Europe, Asia, North America, and Russia. There are 16 subspecies, which include some of the more famous names like the Grizzly, Kodiak, and Eurasian Bear. During the winter months, brown bears hibernate in dens dug out of the soil by using their long claws. Females usually enter their den for hibernation while pregnant with up to three cubs, and give birth while sleeping. The newborn cubs then instinctively crawl into place to nurse from their mother. Emerging from the womb weighing about 1 pound each, they will leave the den in the spring weighing around 20 pounds. The brown bear's diet is widely omnivorous and adapts to the available food during any given season. They feed on berries, grasses, acorns, fungi, insects, grubs, bees, honey, fish, and over 100 different species of mammals, including rodents and bison.

Syrian Brown Bear
(Ursus arctos syriacus)
Found across the Middle East through the Western Himalayas, Syrian Brown Bears are among the smallest of the brown bear subspecies and have a lighter coat than their New World counterparts. They live mostly in high-altitude, mountainous regions.
Length: 55 inches (1.4 meters), head and body
Weight: 550 pounds
Conservation status: Vulnerable

Five claws reaching up to 4 inches (10 centimeters) in length

Paws can reach 16 inches (41 centimeters) in length

Brown Bear Front Paw

Relatively large ears

Thinner build with light brown coloring

Light-colored claws

Massive skull, reaching 25 inches (64 centimeters) in length with enormous teeth

Kodiak Bear
(Ursus arctos middendorffi)
Found in Alaska on Kodiak Island, Kodiak Bears, the largest of all brown bear subspecies, can stand close to 10 feet tall when reared on their hind legs. They are believed to reach this massive size due to the abundance of salmon they eat from May through September.
Length: 8 feet (2.4 meters), head and body
Weight: 1,200 pounds
Conservation status: Least Concern

Grizzly Bear
(Ursus arctos horribilis)
Found in Alaska, Western Canada, and Northwestern United States, Grizzly Bears, also known as North American Brown Bears, were given their name due to their fierce appearance.
Length: 7 feet long (2.1 meters), head and body
Weight: 790 pounds
Conservation status: Least Concern

Large "hump" on back

Longer mane
surrounding head
and ears

Sloth Bear
(*Melursus ursinus*)
Found throughout the Indian
Subcontinent, Sloth Bears are
nocturnal and have specially adapted
lower lips used for sucking up
termites and honeybee colonies.
Length: 6 feet (1.8 meters),
head and body
Weight: 290 pounds
Conservation status: Vulnerable

Long, lanky frame
underneath coat

Long claws used to dig
termite mounds and
find insect grubs

Bears

American Black Bear
(*Ursus americanus*)
Found across the North American Continent, American
Black Bears, despite their name, come in a wide variation
of colors, including white, brown, and black. Opportunistic
feeders, Black Bears will eat discarded carcasses, small
mammals, or insects, but most of their diet is made up of
grasses, nuts, fruits, and berries. American Black Bears are
active both day and night, and are excellent tree climbers.
Length: 79 inches (2 meters), head and body
Weight: 550 pounds
Conservation status: Least Concern

Rounded face

Sense of smell four
times greater than a dog

Short, curved claws
used for climbing

Sun Bear

(Helarctos malayanus)

Found in the tropical forests of Southeast Asia, Sun Bears, also known as Honey Bears, are one of the smallest bear species. They use their long tongue to lap up honey from honeycombs as well as termites, ants and beetle larvae. Excellent climbers, Sun Bears spend a great deal of time in trees where they can reach fruits and figs.

Length: 59 inches (1.4 meters), head and body

Weight: 170 pounds

Conservation status: Vulnerable

Short snout

Small, rounded ears

Unique "U" shaped marking on chest

Large forepaws with enormous curved claws used for digging

Large, powerful frame

Short hind limbs with inward turned paws

Hind legs almost the same length as forelegs

83

Giant Pandas

Giant Pandas, sometimes called Panda Bears, are considered one of the rarest bears in the world. Giant Pandas are almost entirely vegetarian. They spend an average of 14 hours a day eating up to 80 pounds of bamboo shoots and leaves. They occasionally supplement their diet with insects, bird eggs, and small rodents. Baby Giant Pandas are born weighing only 3 to 7 ounces. They grow to about 100 pounds in their first year of life and ultimately reach 900 times their birth weight as adults.

Giant Panda
(Ailuropoda melanoleuca)
Found in South Central China
Length: 6 feet (1.8 meters), head and body
Weight: 350 pounds
Conservation status: Vulnerable

A pseudo-thumb formed from the sesamoid bone in the forepaws allows the Giant Panda to grasp food, much like a hand

Unique black and white markings are present on skin as well as coat

Thick, woolly coat protects from cold temperatures at night

Counting the sesamoid bone, or "thumb," Giant Pandas have 6 toes

Ailuridae

Red Pandas

Although Red Pandas carry a similar name to Giant Pandas, they are not related. Red Pandas are more closely related to raccoons than bears and are the last remaining members of the Ailuridae family. They share much of the same geographic range as Giant Pandas and also eat bamboo shoots and leaves along with fruits, acorns, roots, and eggs. They spend the vast majority of their time in trees, only coming down to forage. They are solitary animals that mark their territories with urine and musk, and they only come in contact with other Red Pandas during mating season.

Red Panda
(Ailurus fulgens)
Found in South Central China
and Eastern Himalayas.
Length: 25 inches (64 centimeters),
head and body
Weight: 25 pounds
Conservation status: Endangered

Pointed ears with tufts of white fur

Red coat of dense fur

Long, furry tail (as long as their full body length) is used as a blanket during cold weather

Dark markings under eyes

Like Giant Pandas, Red Pandas have developed a sixth digit or pseudo-thumb used to grasp bamboo.

Procyonidae

Raccoons, Kinkajous, Coatis

The Procyonidae family of Carnivora consists of medium- to small-sized mammals with ring markings on their tails or distinct markings on their faces. All are omnivorous and most have non-retractable claws, which are used for climbing trees and eating. Procyonidaes are New World animals and inhabit a wide range of environments.

Rounded ears

Small triangular ears

Large, round, forward-facing eyes

Black "mask" across face

Common Raccoon
(Procyon lotor)
Found throughout North America, raccoons are known for their dexterous hands and masked faces. Common Raccoons are a very adaptive species, capable of adjusting to almost any environment. Though primarily nocturnal, raccoons will hunt or forage during the day depending on food availability. Their diet includes worms, insects, and various invertebrates, as well as fruits and nuts.
Length: 28 inches (71 centimeters), head and body
Weight: 20 pounds
Conservation status: Least Concern

Flexible hands

Ringed tail

Raccoons often stand on two legs, but are mostly quadrupeds.

Kinkajou

(Potos flavus)

Found in Central America and northern parts of South America, Kinkajous are tree-dwelling inhabitants of rain forests. Like some new world primates, they have a fully prehensile tail and flexible hands and feet for climbing. Kinkajous eat mostly fruits and will sometimes eat insects and eggs.

Length: 24 inches (61 centimeters), head and body; Weight: 10 pounds

Conservation status: Vulnerable

Covered in a coat of short fur

Furry, banded tail

Prehensile tail acts as fifth limb when climbing

Coatis

Coatis, sometimes called coatimundi, are native to Mexico and Central and South America. They are *diurnal*, or active during the day. There are four species, all with a long snout ending in a pig-like nose, which is used to forage for small insects, spiders, lizards, and eggs.

White-nosed Coati

(Nasua narica)

Found in Mexico and Central America, White-nosed Coatis spend their nighttime hours in trees and come down during the day to search for food.

Length: 22 inches (56 centimeters), head and body

Weight: 20 pounds

Conservation status: Least Concern

Flattened pig-like nose

Mustelidae

Weasels, Badgers, Otters, Ferrets

The Mustelidae family is one of the largest families of Carnivora, containing over 50 species ranging in size from the Giant Otter at 6 feet long (1.8 meters), to the smallest of all Carnivorians, the Least Weasel at 5 to 10 inches (13 to 25 centimeters). Within the diverse variety of forms, there are several features the Mustelidae family share, including long torsos, short legs, reduced and rounded ears, and thick fur. Most are nocturnal, active year-round, and have scent glands used to attract mates or ward off intruders from their territories.

Long neck, same width as head

Short tail

Short legs

Long torso

Least Weasel
(Mustela nivalis)
Found across the globe in the Northern Hemisphere, Least Weasels are voracious hunters capable of taking down bigger prey, such as rabbits. Because of their active life, Least Weasels must consume 40 to 60 percent of their body weight every day.
Length: 5 to 10 inches (13 to 25 centimeters), head and body
Weight: 1 ounce
Conservation status: Least Concern

Large teeth with powerful bite force

Relatively short, thick legs

Wolverine
(Gulo gulo)
Found across the globe in the cold climate areas of the Northern Hemisphere, Wolverines have a well-deserved reputation for being ferocious and are powerful hunter-scavengers armed with a thick hide, a strong bite, and long claws.
Length: 42 inches (1.1 meters), head and body
Weight: 55 pounds
Conservation status: Least Concern

Very large paws with long claws, resembling a bear's

Wide body with stocky build

Wide face with short snout

Low center of gravity

2-inch-long claws for digging

American Badger

(*Taxidea taxus*)

Found in the Western and Central United States, Northern Mexico, and South-Central Canada, American Badgers are solitary and mostly nocturnal hunters. They feed on a wide variety of prey, such as mice, prairie dogs, snakes, skunks, insects, and lizards, as well as corn, sunflower seeds, and honey.

Length: 29 inches (74 centimeters), head and body; Weight: 20 pounds
Conservation status: Least Concern

Black-footed Ferret

(*Mustela nigripes*)

Found in a limited area within Central United States, Black-footed Ferrets spend 90 percent of their time in burrows where they nest and raise their young. Their diet is almost exclusively prairie dogs, but they also are known to eat birds, mice, and lizards.

Length: 21 inches (53 centimeters), head and body
Weight: 3 pounds
Conservation status: Endangered

Black markings around eyes

Thin tail about half the length of torso

Short legs with long digging nails

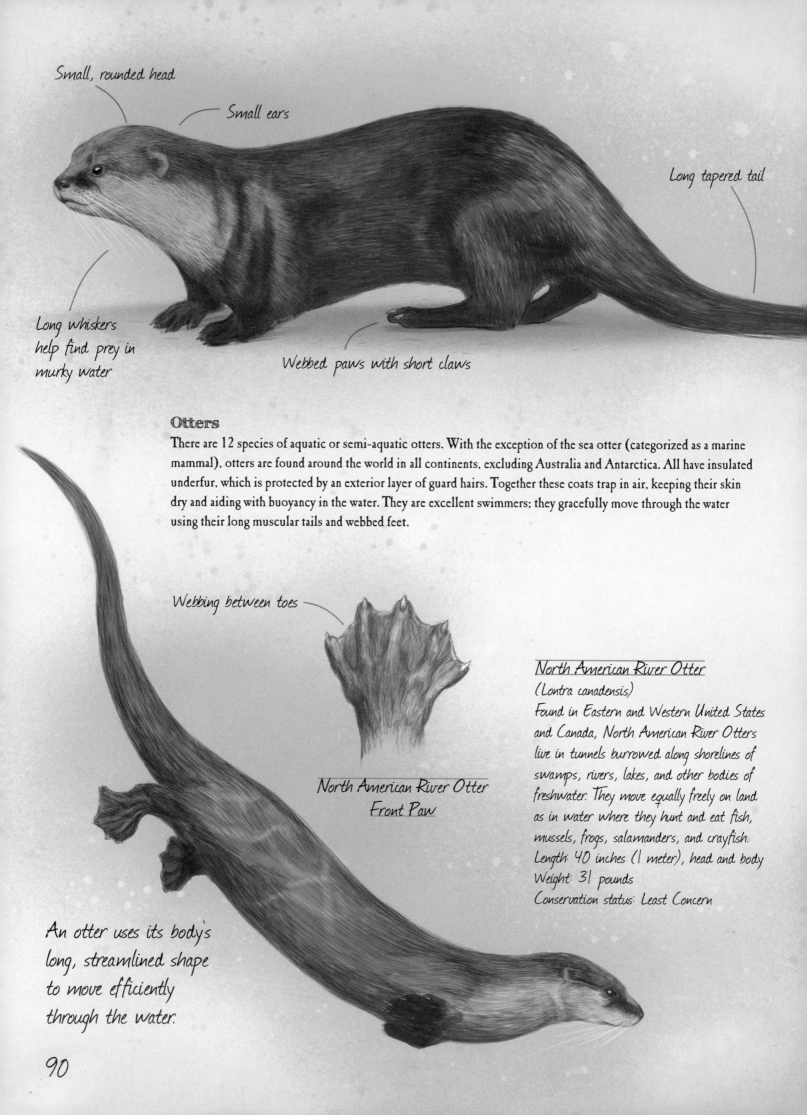

Small, rounded head

Small ears

Long tapered tail

Long whiskers help find prey in murky water

Webbed paws with short claws

Otters

There are 12 species of aquatic or semi-aquatic otters. With the exception of the sea otter (categorized as a marine mammal), otters are found around the world in all continents, excluding Australia and Antarctica. All have insulated underfur, which is protected by an exterior layer of guard hairs. Together these coats trap in air, keeping their skin dry and aiding with buoyancy in the water. They are excellent swimmers; they gracefully move through the water using their long muscular tails and webbed feet.

Webbing between toes

North American River Otter Front Paw

North American River Otter
(Lontra canadensis)
Found in Eastern and Western United States and Canada, North American River Otters live in tunnels burrowed along shorelines of swamps, rivers, lakes, and other bodies of freshwater. They move equally freely on land as in water where they hunt and eat fish, mussels, frogs, salamanders, and crayfish.
Length: 40 inches (1 meter), head and body
Weight: 31 pounds
Conservation status: Least Concern

An otter uses its body's long, streamlined shape to move efficiently through the water.

Mephitidae

Skunks

The Mephitidae family of small mammals includes 12 species of skunks, all of which are known for spraying an unpleasant material from glands underneath their tails when threatened. This secretion has a powerful odor and will sting if it makes contact with eyes. Skunks are nocturnal. They sleep in dens burrowed under rocks, in logs, or under the ground. During the night hours, skunks forage and hunt for food by digging into the ground for insect larvae or grubs and earthworms. They will also eat lizards, frogs, and snakes. Skunks are particularly fond of honeybees, which they hunt by scratching the hive and eating the bees as they emerge from the nest. Their thick coat of fur protects them from bee stings.

At first sight of distress, tail raises to appear larger

Round face with pointed snout

Short, stout body with short legs

Long, curved claws on forepaws

Bushy tail with white ends

Black and white stripes and spotted pattern across back

Striped Skunk
(Mephitis mephitis)
Found throughout the United States, Canada, and Southern Mexico, Striped Skunks are easily identified by the white stripes running across their back and tail. Their coat color can vary from silver to brown to black.
Length: 19 inches (48 centimeters), head and body
Weight: 10 pounds Conservation status: Least Concern

Western Spotted Skunk
(Spilogale gracilis)
Found in Northern Mexico, Western United States, and Western Canada, Western Spotted Skunks stand on their forelimbs with their legs and tail in the air when spraying.
Length: 14 inches (35 centimeters), head and body
Weight: 20 ounces
Conservation status: Least Concern

Eulipotyphla (Shrews, Moles & Hedgehogs)

The Eulipotyphla order of mammals is made up of three families: Soricidae, which includes 300 species of shrews; Talpidae, which includes 42 species of moles; and Erinaceidae, which includes 17 species of hedgehogs. Eulipotyphla mammals feed on invertebrates, insects, earthworms, and plant matter. They are also distinctive in that all have long, pointed, and usually movable snouts, used to locate and secure prey.

Order: Eulipotyphla

Species: Approximately 442

Size Range: 1 inch (2.5 centimeters), Etruscan Shrew, to 10 inches (25 centimeters), European Hedgehog

Weight Range: 2 grams (Etruscan Shrew) to 2 pounds (European Hedgehog)

Distribution: North America, Europe, Asia, and Africa

Habitat: Cold to moderate climates

Facts: For many years, the Eulipotyphla order was categorized as the Insectovra order because of their diets. Ten percent of all land mammal species are part of the Eulipotyphla order.

Erinaceidae

Hedgehogs

Hedgehogs are small nocturnal mammals with spines running across their backs. These spines are used for protection, much like a porcupine's. Unlike porcupines however, hedgehog spines are not barbed and do not easily detach if they come in contact with a predator. When threatened, hedgehogs will roll up into a ball with their spines protruding outward.

<u>European Hedgehog</u>
(Erinaceus europaeus)
Found throughout Europe and parts of Eastern Russia, European Hedgehogs are solitary and live in a wide range of habitats, including meadows, pastures, and even among human settlements.
Length: 10 inches (25 centimeters), head and body; Weight: 2 pounds
Conservation status: Least Concern

Dome-shaped back covered in approximately 6,000 spines

Flat, pig-like nose, giving it its name "hog"

Tiny, hairless tail

Short, strong legs

Talpidae

Moles

Moles are *fossorial* mammals, meaning they are adapted for digging and life underground. Because of their subterranean lifestyle, moles have little use for their eyes. Most mole species have reduced eyes and enlarged forelimbs with long digging claws. They are found in North America, Europe, and Asia.

Star-nosed Mole

(Condylura cristata)
Found in Eastern North America, Star-nosed Moles use the appendages on their noses, called rays, to "see" underground.
Length: 7 inches (18 centimeters), head and body; Weight: 2 ounces
Conservation status: Least Concern

22 flexible appendages cover nostrils when eating

Star-nosed Mole Nose Detail
Star-shaped nose is covered with tiny touch receptors, known as Eimer's organs, that are used to feel surroundings and locate food.

Tiny, underdeveloped eyes with poor vision

Reduced hind limbs

Large forelimbs with digging claws

Soricidae

Shrews

Shrews are small furry mammals resembling mice (though not related) that live in a variety of moist habitats in forests, woods, and grasslands. They include the smallest of all mammal species: the Etruscan Shrew (Suncus etruscus), which reaches only about 1 inch in body length. Shrews are primarily solitary and are extremely active due to a high metabolic rate, causing them to constantly hunt for food. They can be found throughout the world in moderate climates.

Northern Short-tailed Shrew

(Blarina brevicauda)
Found throughout Central and Eastern North America, Northern Short-tailed Shrews are unique in that they are one of the few venomous mammals. The toxin is carried in their saliva and is used to paralyze its prey. Northern Short-tailed Shrews are capable of eating three times their own weight in food daily. They use echolocation to find prey, much like bats do.
Length: 4 inches (10 centimeters), head and body; Weight: 1 ounce
Conservation status: Least Concern

Very small eyes with limited vision

Thick, furry coat of hair

Short tail

Lagomorphs (Rabbits & Pikas)

Lagomorphs resemble rodents in that they both have large incisor teeth used for gnawing. They differ from rodents in that they have four incisors on their upper jaws, whereas rodents only have two. Lagomorphs are represented by 80 species of rabbits, hares, and pikas, all of which are terrestrial.

Order: Lagomorpha

Species: Approximately 80

Size Range: 6 inches (15 centimeters), Northern Pika, to 30 inches (25 centimeters), European Hare

Weight Range: 3.5 ounce (Northern Pika) to 15 pounds (European Hare)

Distribution: All continents except Australia and Antarctica

Habitat: Various conditions, from cold climates in mountainous areas to grasslands

Facts: Until the 20th century, all Lagomorphs were considered rodents.

Rabbits

Rabbits are small mammals in the Leporidae family. Most live in burrows in small groups or colonies in a wide variety of habitats, including woodlands, meadows, grasslands, and deserts. Rabbits can be found in South and North America, Southeast Asia, and Japan. Like their cousins hares, rabbits use their strong hind limbs to propel them by hopping, then softening their landing with their forelimbs.

Eastern Cottontail
(Sylvilagus floridanus)
Found in North America, Eastern Cottontails are one of the most abundant rabbit species in the New World. If pursued, Eastern Cottontails run in a zigzag pattern reaching up to 20 miles per hour (32 kilometers per hour).
Length: 19 inches (48 centimeters), head and body
Weight: 2 pounds
Conservation status: Least Concern

Long, tall ears used to locate threats

Soft, thick fur

White, fluffy tail gives the cottontail its name

Hares

Though similar to rabbits, hares differ in that they give birth to babies, called kits, that are fully covered in hair and able to see. In contrast, rabbit kits are born blind and hairless. Hares are also generally larger and live solitary lives as compared to rabbits. There are 32 species of hares belonging to the Lepus family.

Cape Hare

(Lepus capensis)
Found in Africa, Arabia, and India, Cape Hares inhabit arid areas from coastal plains to mountains. They are nocturnal and feed primarily on grasses and shrubs.
Length: 22 inches
(56 centimeters), head and body
Weight: 4 pounds
Conservation status:
Least Concern

Tall ears with black markings on tips

Large eyes with good peripheral vision

Hind limbs much longer than forelimbs

Pikas

Pikas are the smallest of the Lagomorphs, reaching only about 9 inches. They can be found in North America, Eastern Europe, and Asia in high-altitude, mountainous areas. (They prefer rocky slopes.) Pikas are herbivores—they eat grasses, mosses, twigs, and lichen. They form social groups and use a series of high pitch vocalizations to communicate warnings or to let others know where they are. There are 30 species of Pikas.

Rounded ears

Squat, oval-shaped torso

Short legs with low center of gravity

American Pika

(Ochotona princeps)
Found in Northwestern United States and Southwestern Canada, American Pikas are diurnal, or active during the day. They make their home in piles of rock or fallen timber, where they hoard food for the winter months.
Length: 8 inches (20 centimeters), head and body
Weight: 6 ounces
Conservation status: Least Concern

Perissodactyls (Odd-toed Ungulates)

Odd-toed ungulates belong to the order Perissodactyla and are characterized by having an odd number of toes or hooves on their feet. They are also distinguishable by their simple, single-chambered stomachs in which they digest only plant matter consisting mostly of grasses, leaves, and other plant parts. The Perissodactyla order is divided into three families: Equidae, including horses, zebras, and donkeys; Tapiridae, including tapirs; and Rhinocerotidae, including rhinoceroses.

Order: Perissodactyla

Species: 17

Size Range: 51 inches (1.3 meters), Kabomani Tapir, to 14 feet (4.2 meters), White Rhinoceros

Weight Range: 240 pounds (Kabomani Tapir) to 5,000 pounds (White Rhinoceros)

Distribution: Central and South America, Eastern and Southern Africa, and Central and Southern Asia

Habitat: Tropical rain forests, dry savannas, and open grasslands

Facts: The White Rhinoceros is the second largest land mammal after the elephant.
Zebras are actually black with white stripes, not white with black stripes.

Zebra foot

Tapir foot

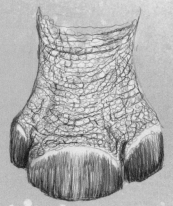

Rhinoceros foot

<u>Odd-toed Ungulate Hooves</u>
Perissodactyla feet are composed of either one or three hooves, with the exception of the tapir's forefeet, which have a fourth hoof that does not touch the ground. The bulk of the animal's weight is carried on the larger center hoof with the outside toes used for support.

Equidae

Donkeys

The Equidae family of ungulates contains many well-known members, including horses, donkeys, and zebras, all of which have a single toe or hoof on each foot. They are from Africa, Arabia, the Middle East, and Central Asia. Many species, like horses, were brought to the New World where they established themselves in the wild. There are a total of 7 species in the Equidae family and all of them fall under the genus *Equus*.

African Wild Donkey

(*Equus africanus*)

Found in the African countries of Eritrea, Ethiopia, and Somalia, African wild donkeys are believed to be the ancestor of the domestic donkey. They once roamed a much larger area in Africa, but now they are found in very few remaining areas, with just over only 500 individuals left in the wild. They feed on grasses and leaves.

Length: 66 inches (1.6 meters), head and body

Weight: 600 pounds

Conservation status: Critically Endangered

Upright mane with dark tips

Long, barrel-shaped torso

Long, narrow head with large ears

Short tail with tuft of hair at the end

Shorter, stockier legs than domesticated horses, with pale striped markings

Zebras

Zebras collectively consist of three species: the Mountain Zebra, Plains Zebra, and Grévy's Zebra. Each species has its own distinct pattern of stripes, much like fingerprints. It is believed that their black and white markings are used to confuse predators that are approaching a herd by making it difficult to select one individual. Zebras are social animals that travel in groups of one male and several females. These groups unite to form herds of thousands, giving them protection in numbers. Zebras feed almost exclusively on grasses and sleep standing up and take turns keeping watch for predators.

Grant's Zebra

(Equus quagga boehmi)
Found in sub-Saharan and Eastern Africa, Grant's Zebras are a subspecies of the Plains Zebras (Equus quagga), also known as the Common Zebra. They are distinguished from the other subspecies in that they are part of the Serengeti-Mara ecosystem. Grant's Zebras have a broader stripe pattern than other species.
Length: 7 Feet (2.1 meters), head and body
Weight: 660 pounds
Conservation status: Least Concern

Stripes continue onto mane

Short tail

Markings fade on legs, with ankles entirely white

Legs are shorter than other Zebra species

Dark hooves

Grévy's Zebra

(Equus grevyi)

Found in Kenya and Ethiopia, Grévy's Zebras are the largest of all the zebra species. They are known for the tight, intricate pattern reaching down to their ankles. They are unique from other species of zebra in that they do not form groups; they form few social bonds with others.

Length: 9 Feet (2.7 meters), head and body)
Weight: 990 pounds
Conservation status: Endangered

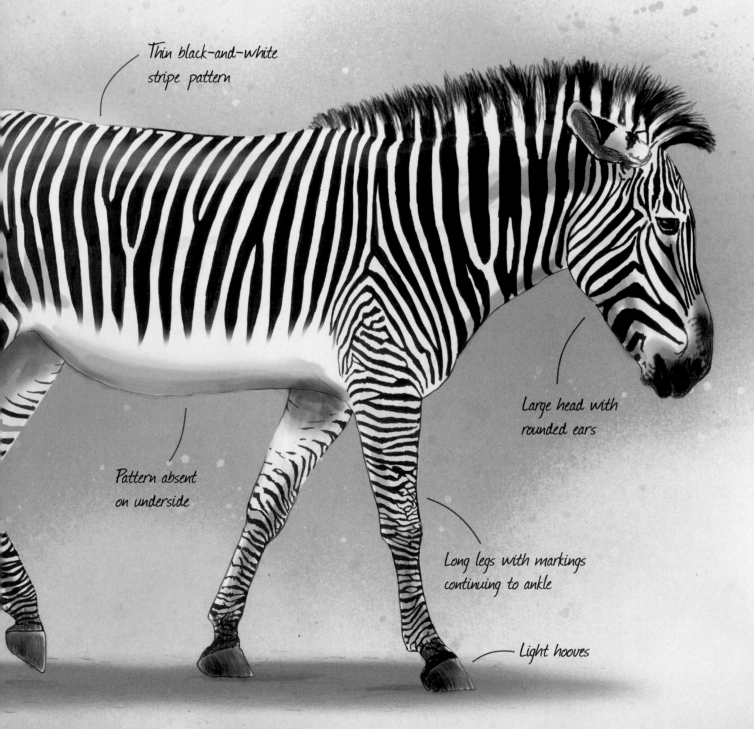

Thin black-and-white stripe pattern

Pattern absent on underside

Large head with rounded ears

Long legs with markings continuing to ankle

Light hooves

Tapiridae

Tapirs

Tapirs are known for being large and having a short, prehensile trunk. There are a total of five species, with four of them found in South America and one in Asia. Tapirs spend time in dry forests but are commonly found near and around bodies of freshwater, where they swim to keep cool and feed on aquatic vegetation. They also eat fruits, berries, and leaves, eating up to 85 pounds of vegetation a day. Tapirs are mostly nocturnal and have few predators due to their size and the thickness of their skin.

Malayan Tapir
(Tapirus indicus)

Found in Indonesia, Thailand, and Malaysia, Malayan Tapirs are easily recognizable due to their distinct black and white "saddle" markings. They are the largest of the tapir species and the only surviving member from Asia. Malayan Tapirs live in dense rain forests where they use their acute sense of smell to find fruits and leaves.

Length: 8.5 feet (2.6 meters), head and body
Weight: 1,000 pounds
Conservation status: Endangered

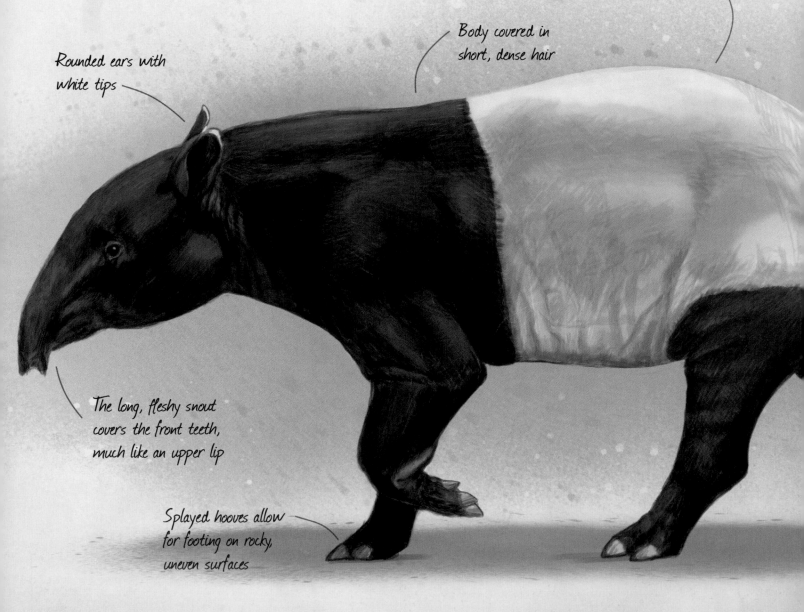

"Saddle" markings on all adults

Body covered in short, dense hair

Rounded ears with white tips

The long, fleshy snout covers the front teeth, much like an upper lip

Splayed hooves allow for footing on rocky, uneven surfaces

Their very flexible prehensile snout is used to reach for leaves or branches while feeding. Tapirs are commonly seen raising their trunk and bearing their teeth when trying to detect a scent. This posture is called the "flehmen response."

42 to 44 teeth used to cut and grind plant matter

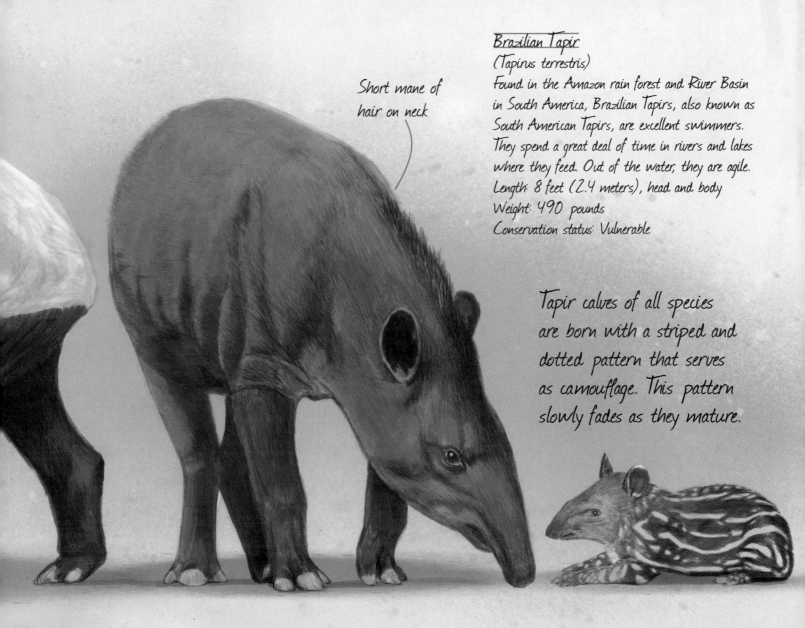

Short mane of hair on neck

Brazilian Tapir
(Tapirus terrestris)
Found in the Amazon rain forest and River Basin in South America, Brazilian Tapirs, also known as South American Tapirs, are excellent swimmers. They spend a great deal of time in rivers and lakes where they feed. Out of the water, they are agile.
Length: 8 feet (2.4 meters), head and body
Weight: 490 pounds
Conservation status: Vulnerable

Tapir calves of all species are born with a striped and dotted pattern that serves as camouflage. This pattern slowly fades as they mature.

Rhinoceros

Rhinoceroses

Rhinoceroses are identifiable by their size and the enormous horns growing from their heads. They are the second largest of all land mammals (after the elephant) and are comprised of five species: two in Africa (the White Rhinoceros and the Black Rhinoceros) and three in Asia (the Javan, Indian, and Sumatran Rhinoceroses). Rhinoceroses' horns are made of keratin, the same material fingernails are made of, not of bone. They use their horns to fight one another during courtship and as self-defense. Unfortunately, rhinoceroses are hunted for their horns, which is causing their endangerment.

White Rhinoceros
(Ceratotherium simum)
Found in Southern Africa, White Rhinoceroses are the largest of all rhinoceros species. Though the name "white" does not represent their color, it is believed to be a mispronunciation from Dutch meaning "wide." This refers to the wide, square appearance of their mouths.
Length: 13 feet (3.9 meters), head and body
Weight: 5,000 pounds
Conservation status: Near Threatened

Head held upright for feeding on leaves from low branches

Long, pointed horn can reach up to 50 inches in length

Head positioned low with square, wide lips designed for feeding on grasses

Thick, short, powerful legs

Black Rhinoceros

(Diceros bicornis)

Found in Southeastern Africa, Black Rhinoceroses were named to differentiate them from the White Rhinoceros, not as a reference to their color. They share many of the same habitats as the White Rhinoceros. They differ in that they have triangular-shaped lips designed to pull leaves from trees.

Length: 12 feet (3.6 meters), head and body

Weight: 3,000 pounds

Conservation status: Critically Endangered

Indian Rhinoceros

(Rhinoceros unicornis)

Found in the northern Indian subcontinent, Indian Rhinoceroses, also called Greater One-horned Rhinoceros, are the second largest species, distinguishable from their African counterparts by the thick, bumpy armor surrounding their torsos. They also have only one horn.

Length: 12.5 feet (3.8 meters), head and body

Weight: 4,800 pounds

Conservation status: Vulnerable

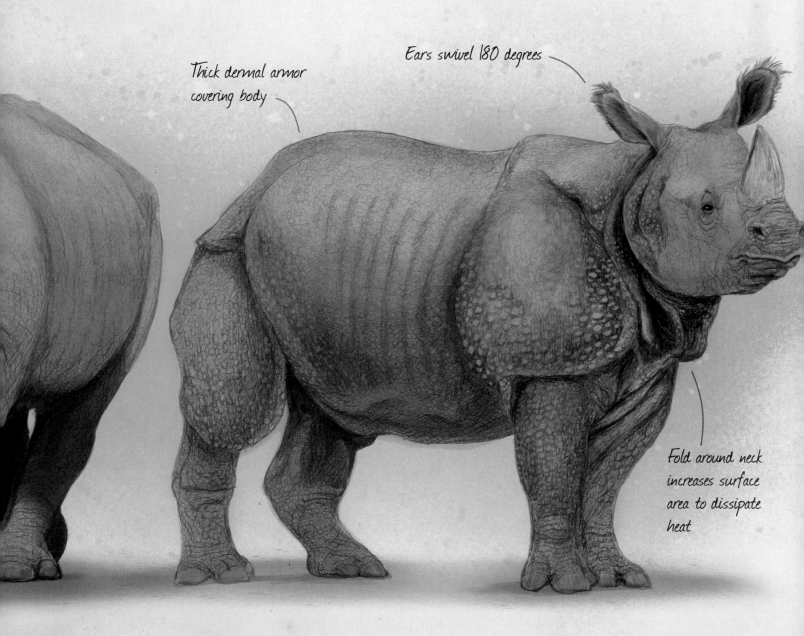

Thick dermal armor covering body

Ears swivel 180 degrees

Fold around neck increases surface area to dissipate heat

Rodentia (Rodents)

One of the largest orders of land mammals, rodents are characterized by having two long incisor teeth on both the top and bottom jaws. These teeth never stop growing; they require the grinding of constant use to keep from overgrowing. Rodents generally have acute sight, smell, and hearing senses, which are used to both gather food and flee predators. All have long whiskers called *vibrissae* used as an additional sensory organ to feel the area around their mouths. Rodents can be broken down into three groups; Myomorpha for mouse-like rodents, Sciuromorpha for squirrel-like rodents, and Hystricomorpha for porcupine-like rodents.

Order: Rodentia

Species: Approximately 2,277

Size Range: 1.7 inches (4.3 centimeters), Baluchistan Pygmy Jerboa, to 4 feet (1.2 meters), Capybara

Weight Range: .132 ounce (Baluchistan Pygmy Jerboa) to 146 pounds (Capybara)

Distribution: All continents, with the exception of Antarctica

Habitat: Almost all habitats, from frozen tundras to dry deserts

Facts: Forty percent of all mammal species are rodents. Rodents have adapted to almost every terrestrial habitat, including human habitats.

Mice

Characterized as small with pointed noses and long hairless tails, mice are divided into two families: Old World mice and New World mice. There are over 100 species.

Rats

Though rat is a term loosely used to identify small- to medium-sized rodents, true rats belong to the family Rattus. There are approximately 70 members of this family. Rats have an extremely varied diet and eat almost any organic material.

Small, rounded ears

Wood Mouse
(Apodemus sylvaticus)
Found in Europe and Northwestern Africa.
Length: 3.5 inches (8.9 centimeters),
head and body
Weight: .5 ounce
Conservation status: Least Concern

Brown Rat
(Rattus norvegicus)
Found on all continents except Antarctica.
Length: 8 inches (20 centimeters),
head and body
Weight: 12 ounces
Conservation status: Least Concern

Long, hairless tail

Myomorpha (Mouse-like Rodents)

Myomorpha rodents are typically small and have jaw structures and muscles designed for gnawing. This group includes mice, rats, hamsters, gerbils, gophers, and voles. The Myomorpha suborder consists of about 1,100 species in total.

Vibrissae, or whiskers, used to sense area around mouth and to find food

Long incisor teeth are the defining characteristic of rodents

Jerboas

Known for jumping like kangaroos, jerboas are nocturnal desert dwellers that spend the hot daylight hours in burrows, only coming out at night. They feed on grass, leaves, and soft seeds.

Four-toed Jerboa
(Allactaga tetradactyla)
Found in Egypt and Libya in dry desert environments.
Length: 8 inches (20 centimeters), head and body
Weight: 6 ounces
Conservation status: Vulnerable

Gophers

Gophers are small burrowing mammals. Also known as pocket gophers, they mostly have brown fur, which matches the color of the soil and camouflages them from predators.

Botta's Pocket Gopher
(Thomomys bottae)
Found in Western North America, Botta's Pocket Gophers spend most of their time in burrows dug with their teeth. Their burrows can reach up to 5 feet deep and have multiple chambers for eating and sleeping.
Length: 10.5 inches (27 centimeters), head and body
Weight: 12 ounces
Conservation status: Least Concern

Large teeth for body size

Large ears

Long, powerful legs used for jumping

Short, hairless tail

Sciuromorpha (Squirrel-like Rodents)

The Sciuromorpha suborder of rodents includes three families: Sciuridae, Aplodontiidae, and Gliridae. They share similar skull structures and muscle attachments in their jaws. Sciuromorpha range in size from the African Pygmy Squirrel at 3 inches (7.5 centimeters) in length to the North American Beaver at 35 inches (89 centimeters) in length.

Horizontal stripes with two darker markings and one lighter in between

Short tail

Chipmunks

Chipmunks belong to the genus *Tamias*, which are known for storing food and dispersing seeds within their habitats. They forage on the ground and climb trees to find food, mostly seeds, nuts, and fruits, but they also consume insects, small frogs, and bird eggs.

Eastern Chipmunk
(*Tamias striatus*)
Found in Eastern North America, Eastern Chipmunks live in wooded areas and favor rocky terrain, where they can find cover to evade predators.
Length: 6 inches (15 centimeters), head and body
Weight: 5 ounces
Conservation status: Least Concern

Large, bushy tail measuring the full length of the body

Large eyes with great peripheral vision

Squirrels

With the exception of marmots, squirrels are mostly *arboreal*, or tree-dwelling rodents. They feed primarily on seeds and nuts, but also supplement their diet with insects and small reptiles. There are 285 species of squirrels.

Flexible ankle joints allowing for 180-degree rotation

Eastern Gray Squirrel
(*Sciurus carolinensis*)
Found in Eastern North America, Eastern Gray Squirrels are crepuscular, or mostly active in the early morning and late afternoon. They use their tail for communication by twitching it to warn others of danger. If caught while fleeing a predator, their skin, hair, or vertebrae can break off to avoid capture.
Length: 11 inches (28 centimeters), head and body; Weight: 20 ounces
Conservation status: Least Concern

Bulky body with short legs

Short, bushy tail

Marmots

The 15 species of marmots belong to the squirrel family, including groundhogs and ground squirrels. They are fully terrestrial and inhabit mountainous areas. Marmots typically live in burrows and are highly social. They use whistle-like vocalizations to communicate, giving them the nickname "whistle pigs."

Yellow-bellied Marmot
(Marmota flaviventris)
Found in the Western United States and Southwestern Canada, Marmots feed on grasses, grains, grasshoppers, and bird eggs.
Length: 20 inches (51 centimeters), head and body
Weight: 11 pounds
Conservation status: Least Concern

Teeth contain iron, making them appear orange

Beavers

Beavers are the largest of the Sciuromorpha group of rodents and are represented by two species: the North American Beaver and the Eurasian Beaver. They are known for their semi-aquatic lifestyle and their powerful jaw and teeth, which are used to cut down trees. They build dams to protect themselves from predators and as a means of storing food. Beavers are highly social mammals.

North American Beaver
(Castor canadensis)
Found in the United States and Canada, North American Beavers feed on grasses, barks, aquatic plants, and ferns.
Length: 35 inches (89 centimeters), head and body
Weight: 80 pounds
Conservation status: Least Concern

Waterproof coat of fur

Long, flattened, paddle-like tail used to aid in swimming

Hystricomorpha (Porcupine-like Rodents)

The Hystricomorpha group of rodents is represented by 230 species, including some of the largest rodents, such as the capybara. Not all Hystricomorphs are large—some are small like guinea pigs, mole rats, and chinchillas. Hystricomorphs are found throughout North and South America, Africa, and Asia.

Agoutis

Agoutis are large rodents found in Central and South America. They are terrestrial, very fast runners, and capable of jumping 6 feet in the air to evade predators.

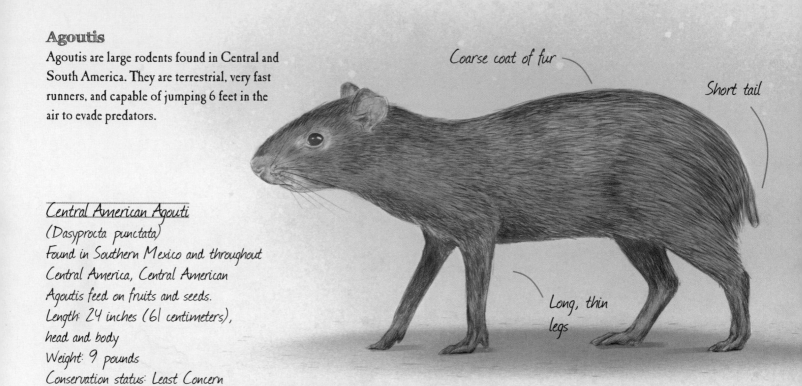

Coarse coat of fur

Short tail

Long, thin legs

Central American Agouti

(Dasyprocta punctata)
Found in Southern Mexico and throughout Central America, Central American Agoutis feed on fruits and seeds.
Length: 24 inches (61 centimeters), head and body
Weight: 9 pounds
Conservation status: Least Concern

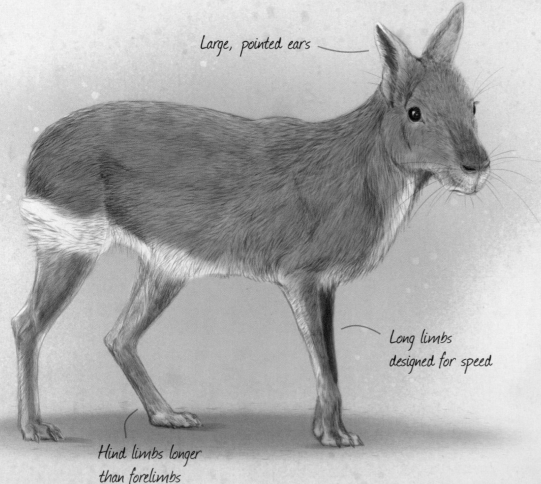

Large, pointed ears

Maras

Maras resemble a mixture of a rabbit with a deer, but are not related to either. They belong to the Cavy family and are the fourth largest rodent after the capybara, porcupine, and beaver.

Patagonian Mara

(Dolichotis patagonum)
Found in Southwestern Argentina, Patagonian Maras feed primarily on vegetation and fruits.
Length: 30 inches (76 centimeters), head and body
Weight: 35 pounds
Conservation status: Near Threatened

Long limbs designed for speed

Hind limbs longer than forelimbs

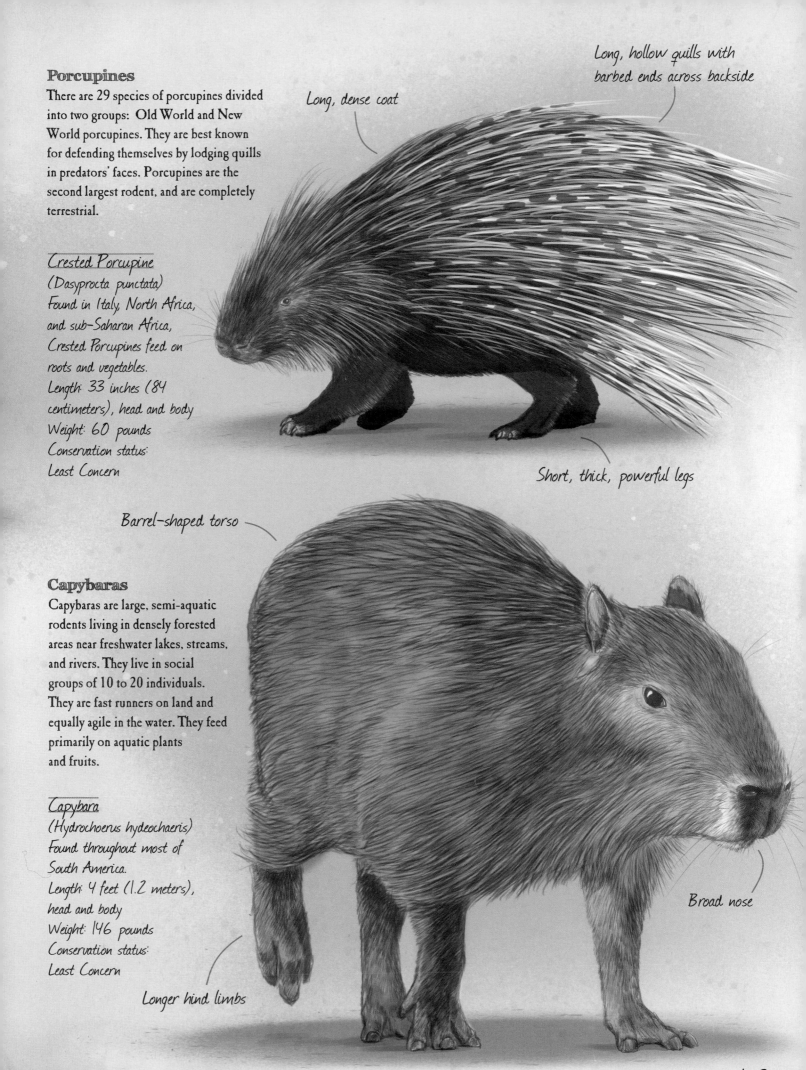

Porcupines

There are 29 species of porcupines divided into two groups: Old World and New World porcupines. They are best known for defending themselves by lodging quills in predators' faces. Porcupines are the second largest rodent, and are completely terrestrial.

Crested Porcupine

(Dasyprocta punctata)
Found in Italy, North Africa, and sub-Saharan Africa, Crested Porcupines feed on roots and vegetables.
Length: 33 inches (84 centimeters), head and body
Weight: 60 pounds
Conservation status: Least Concern

Long, dense coat

Long, hollow quills with barbed ends across backside

Short, thick, powerful legs

Barrel-shaped torso

Capybaras

Capybaras are large, semi-aquatic rodents living in densely forested areas near freshwater lakes, streams, and rivers. They live in social groups of 10 to 20 individuals. They are fast runners on land and equally agile in the water. They feed primarily on aquatic plants and fruits.

Capybara

(Hydrochoerus hydeochaeris)
Found throughout most of South America.
Length: 4 feet (1.2 meters), head and body
Weight: 146 pounds
Conservation status: Least Concern

Longer hind limbs

Broad nose

109

Proboscidea (Elephants)

The largest of all land mammals, elephants are represented by two species: the African Elephant and the Asian Elephant, both belonging to the Proboscidea family. Aside from their enormous size, elephants' trunks are their most recognizable feature. Made up of over 30,000 muscles, their trunks are extremely flexible and versatile. They are used for everything, from picking up food and drinking water to caressing their young. Elephants are highly social and very intelligent and are capable of expressing emotions such as empathy, sorrow, and happiness. Females, or cows, form family groups with their young and other related females, numbering up to 10 members led by a matriarch, usually the oldest female. Elephants are herbivores, eating mostly grasses, fruits, and leaves, and can consume several hundred pounds of plant material daily.

Order: Proboscidea

Species: 2

Size Range: 20 feet (6 meters), Asian Elephant, to 24 feet (7.3 meters), African Elephant

Weight Range: 6,000 pounds (Asian Elephant) to 13,000 pounds (African Elephant)

Distribution: Sub-Saharan Africa, South Asia, and Southeast Asia

Habitat: Deserts, forests, savannas, and marshes

Facts: The elephant's closest living relatives are manatees, marine mammals.

A newborn elephant weighs 230 pounds. Elephants are the only mammal that cannot jump or lift all four feet off the ground.

Asian Elephants
Found in Southeastern Asia and the smaller of the two species, Asian Elephants' tusks are usually only found on males. (Females rarely grow smaller tusks.) Their tusks are used as weapons, as well as to dig for water and uproot trees. Elephants generally favor one tusk over the other, making them either left- or right-"handed."

Trunk is commonly used to bring food to mouth and can carry up to 600 pounds

Absence of tusks

Asian Elephants have one prehensile tip at the end of their trunks called a "finger."

Female Asian Elephant

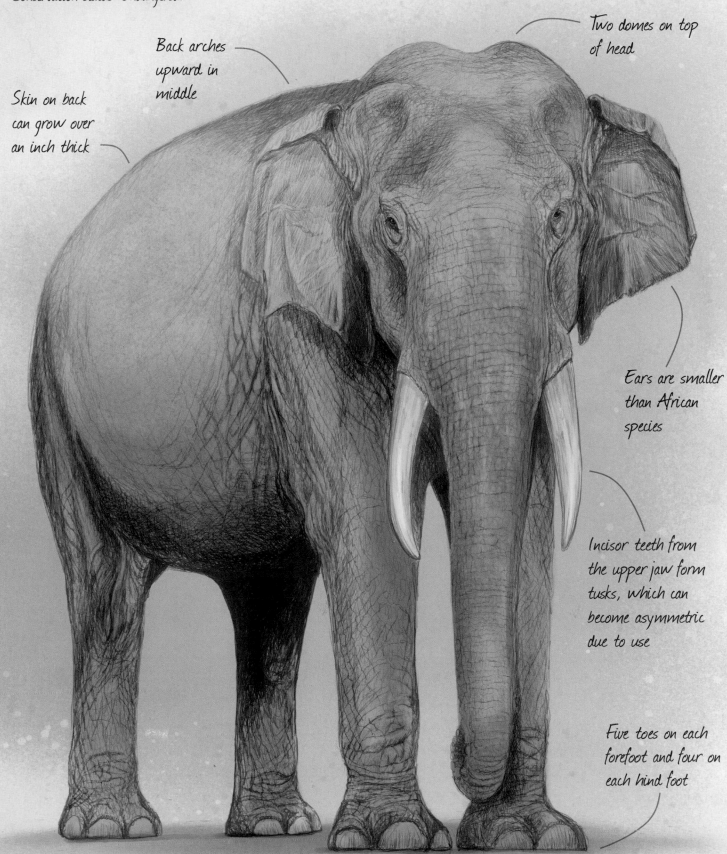

Male Asian Elephant
(Elephas maximus)
Length: 20 feet (6 meters), head and body
Weight: 6,000 pounds
Conservation status: Endangered.

Back arches
upward in
middle

Skin on back
can grow over
an inch thick

Two domes on top
of head

Ears are smaller
than African
species

Incisor teeth from
the upper jaw form
tusks, which can
become asymmetric
due to use

Five toes on each
forefoot and four on
each hind foot

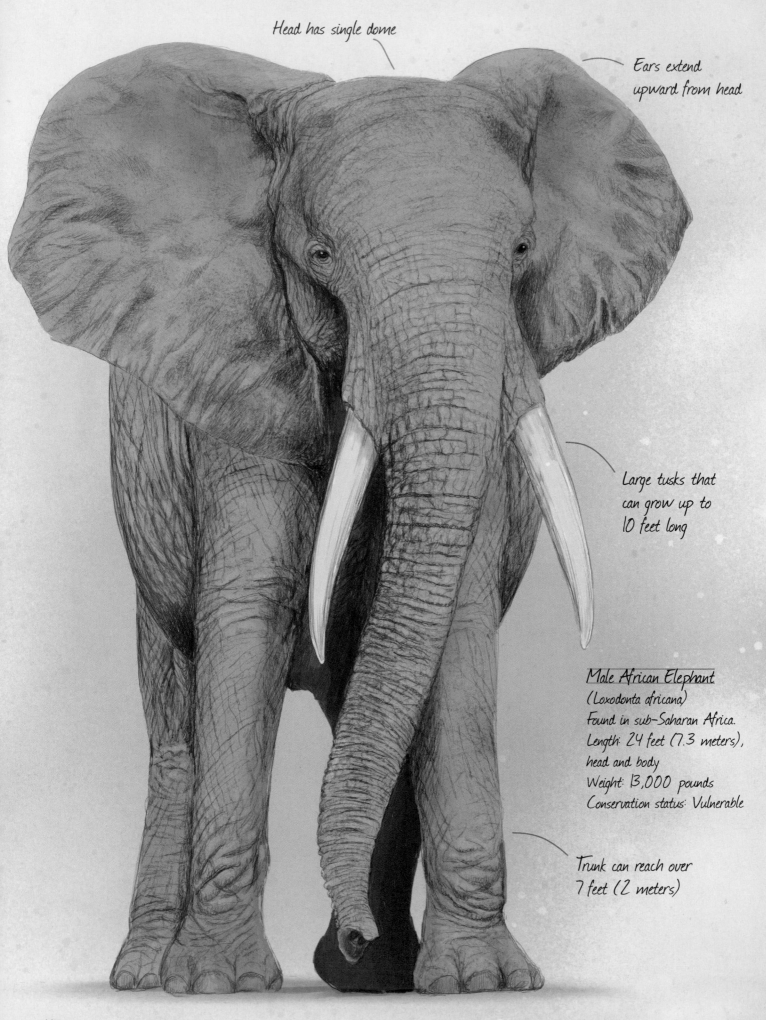

Head has single dome

Ears extend
upward from head

Large tusks that
can grow up to
10 feet long

Male African Elephant
(Loxodonta africana)
Found in sub-Saharan Africa.
Length: 24 feet (7.3 meters),
head and body
Weight: 13,000 pounds
Conservation status: Vulnerable

Trunk can reach over
7 feet (2 meters)

African Elephants

African Elephants are the largest of land mammals. They can be distinguished from Asian Elephants by their enormous ears, which are used to regulate their body temperature through a network of blood vessels. Sometimes the African heat is too much, so they are never too far from a water source, where they can bathe to keep cool. Elephants are excellent swimmers and at times use their trunks as snorkels when submerged. Female African Elephants grow tusks like the males, though the males' are usually thicker.

African Elephants have two "fingers" at the tips of their trunks, which are dexterous enough to pick up a single berry from the ground.

Female African Elephant

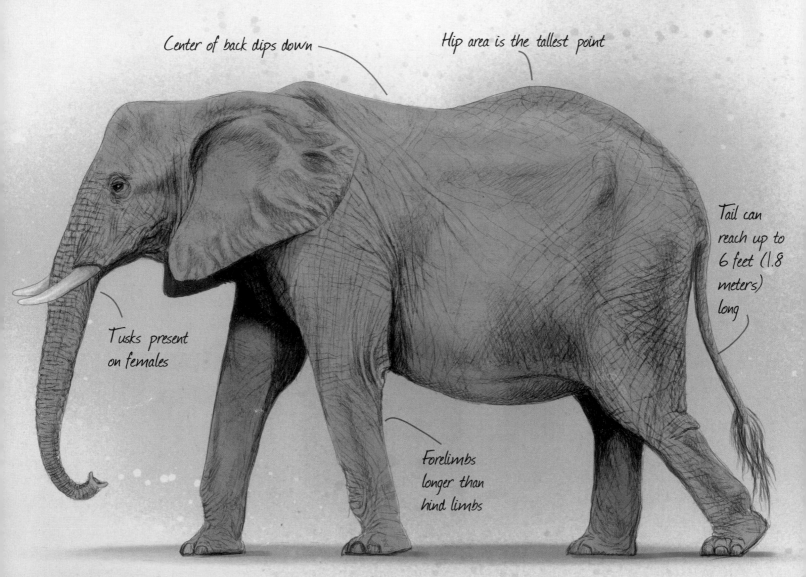

Center of back dips down

Hip area is the tallest point

Tail can reach up to 6 feet (1.8 meters) long

Tusks present on females

Forelimbs longer than hind limbs

Artiodactyla (Even-toed Ungulates)

As their name implies, even-toed ungulates are characterized by having an even number of toes or hooves on each foot. Mostly herbivorous, all even-toed ungulates have multi-chambered stomachs used to ferment and process plant matter. Pigs, cows, and goats are all members of this family. Even-toed ungulates belong to the Artiodactyla order, which is comprised of three suborders and 10 families.

Order: Artiodactyla

Species: Approximately 220

Size Range: 18 inches (46 centimeters), Lesser Mouse-Deer, to 18 feet (5.4 meters), Masai Giraffe

Weight Range: 16 pounds (Lesser Mouse-Deer) to 4,000 pounds (Common Hippopotamus)

Distribution: All continents except Antarctica and Australia (introduced to Australia by humans)

Habitat: Almost all habitats, including arctic tundras, tropical rain forests, arid deserts, and open grasslands

Facts: Cetaceans, or whales, are related to even-toed ungulates. Almost all even-toed ungulate species have weapons consisting of either horns, antlers or tusks.

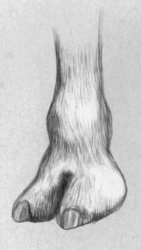

Camel Foot

Warthog Foot

Giraffe Foot

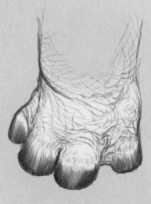

Hippopotamus Foot

Even-toed Ungulate Hooves

Artiodactylas' feet are composed of either two or four hooves. The animal's weight is distributed over the two center hooves equally. The hooves are adapted for specific terrains, from traveling through sand to wading through water.

Camelidae

Camels

There are eight species in the Camelidae family of ungulates, including camels, llamas, and alpacas. All members of the Camelidae family are strictly herbivorous, feeding on grasses and various plants. Camelids have developed adaptations for life in harsh environments, such as fat reserves and thick coats of fur. While most even-toed ungulates have hooves, Camelidae are one of the only families with toenails.

<u>Dromedary Camel</u>
(Camelus dromedarius)
Found in Saharan Africa, the Middle East, and now Australia. Dromedary Camels have a large, single hump on their backs used as fat storage. This species has become entirely domesticated and has not existed in the wild for over 2,000 years.
Length: 10 feet (3 meters), head and body
Weight: 1,320 pounds
Conservation status: Data Deficient

Two humps on back

Single hump on back

Thick coat of hair

<u>Bactrian Camel</u>
(Camelus bactrianus)
Found in Central Asia, Bactrian Camels are easily identified by their two humps used for fat storage. They have been completely domesticated. The few that remain in the wild are classified under the species name Camelus ferus.
Length: 11.5 feet (3.5 meters), head and body
Weight: 2,200 pounds
Conservation status: Data Deficient

Short, stocky legs

Long, thin legs

Broad, rounded feet for walking on sand

Two toes with small toenails

Suidae

Pigs, Hogs, and Boars

The Suidae family consists of 16 species of pigs, hogs, and boars, all characterized by having large heads and torsos, short legs, four-toed feet (two make contact with the ground), and round distinctive noses. Suids are generally smart animals with a well-developed sense of hearing and an acute sense of smell. Females give birth to large litters, reaching up to 12 piglets, and travel with their young in groups called *sounders*. Males are mostly solitary. Suids inhabit forested areas, with exception of the warthog, which lives in the African savanna.

Red River Hog
(*Potamochoerus porcus*)
Found in forests in Central Africa, Red River Hogs are primarily nocturnal and omnivorous, eating mainly tubers and roots. They will supplement their diet with grasses, as well as scavenged dead animals. They are named for their reddish, orange coat.
Length: 5 feet (1.5 meters), head and body
Weight: 260 pounds
Conservation status: Least Concern

Common Warthog
(*Phacochoerus africanus*)
Found in the savanna grasslands in sub-Saharan Africa, Common Warthogs have prominent tusks, which are used for digging and self-defense. The upper tusks grow increasingly curved as it matures. The lower tusks are much sharper and capable of inflicting injury. Common Warthogs eat a varied diet depending on the season that includes grasses, roots, fruits, and carrion.
Length: 56 inches (1.4 meters), head and body
Weight: 330 pounds
Conservation status: Least Concern

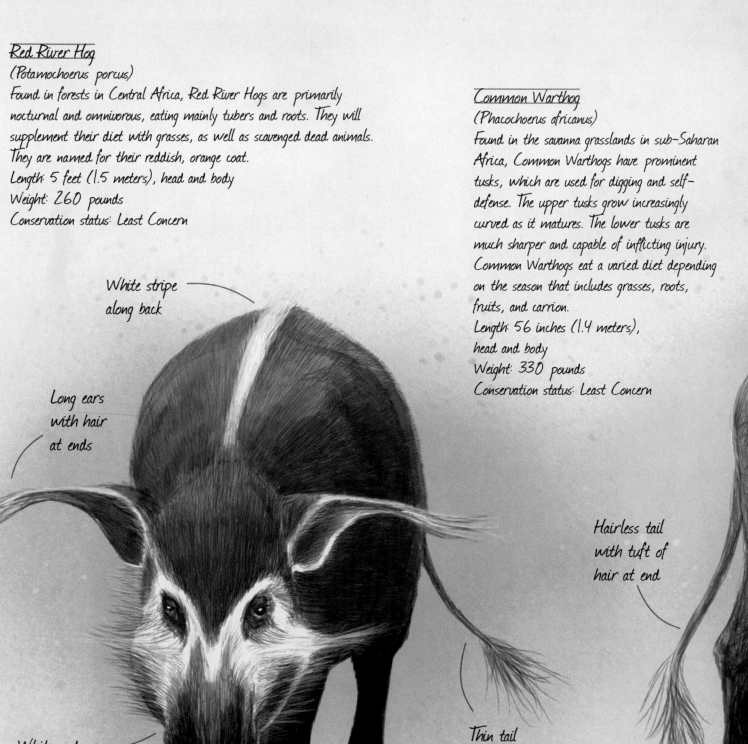

White stripe along back

Long ears with hair at ends

Hairless tail with tuft of hair at end

Thin tail

White and black markings on face

Curved tusks protruding
from skull

<u>North Sulawesi Babirusa</u>
(*Babyrousa celebensis*)
Found in Indonesia, North Sulawesi Babirusas
are unmistakable—their large, curved tusks can
reach 12 inches long. Only growing on males,
the tusks are comprised of both sets of canine
teeth. The upper pair grows from the top
jaw, protrudes through the skin, and curves
backward towards their head. The lower pair
grows from their lower jaw.
Length: 43 inches (1.1 meters), head and body
Weight: 220 pounds
Conservation status: Vulnerable

Long tusks from bottom jaw

Mane of wiry black hair

Cheek pads
called "warts"
on sides of head

Two sets of
large tusks

Hippopotamidae

Hippopotamuses

The Hippopotamidae family is represented by two species, the Common Hippopotamus and the Pygmy Hippopotamus. They spend most of their time in freshwater rivers and other bodies of water, and are the closest living relatives to Cetaceans, or whales. Hippopotamuses have large bodies with large heads, broad mouths, and stand on small stubby legs. Unlike other even-toed ungulates, hippopotamuses don't have hair covering their bodies, and they don't have sweat glands to keep them cool. Their stomachs are divided into three chambers designed to digest plants exclusively. Hippopotamuses' tusks are actually canine teeth that never stop growing throughout their lives, and are completely concealed when their mouths are closed.

Pygmy Hippopotamus
(Choeropsis liberiensis)
Found in Western Africa, Pygmy Hippopotamuses are primarily solitary animals, hiding during the daytime in rivers and emerging at dusk to feed on broad-leafed plants and fruits. Unlike their larger cousins, the Common Hippopotamus, Pygmy Hippopotamuses are not aggressive and spend more time out of the water.
Length: 5 feet (1.5 meters), head and body
Weight: 600 pounds
Conservation status: Endangered

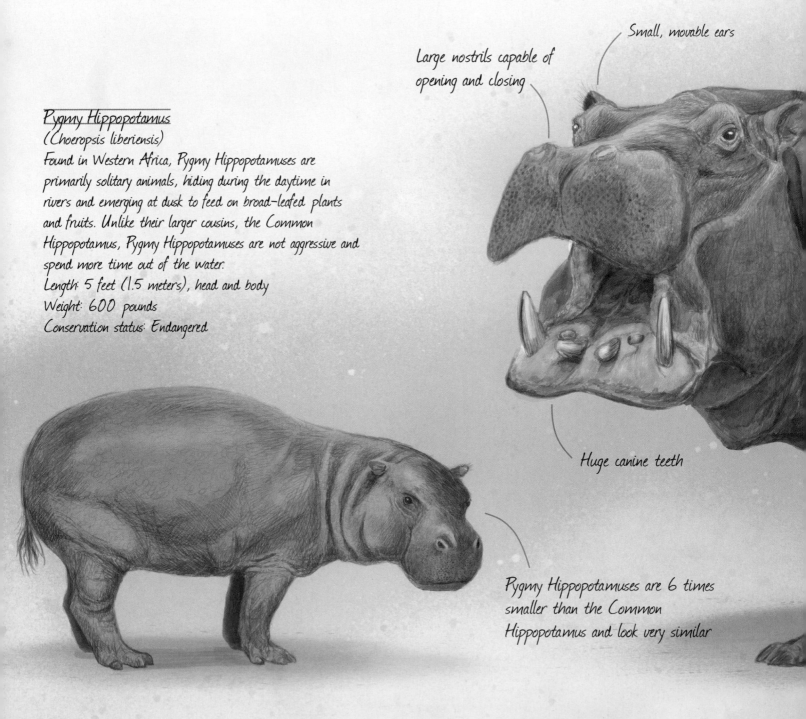

Large nostrils capable of opening and closing

Small, movable ears

Huge canine teeth

Pygmy Hippopotamuses are 6 times smaller than the Common Hippopotamus and look very similar

Common Hippopotamus
(Hippopotamus amphibius)

Found in the southern African continent, Common Hippopotamuses are designed for living submerged in the water. Their eyes, ears, and nostrils are arranged high on their skulls. They only leave the water at night, and travel up to 6 miles to find grass and other plant matter to feed on. Common Hippopotamuses are extremely territorial and aggressive, and are considered to be one of the most dangerous mammals in Africa.

Length: 15 feet (4.5 meters), head and body

Weight: 4,000 pounds

Conservation status: Vulnerable

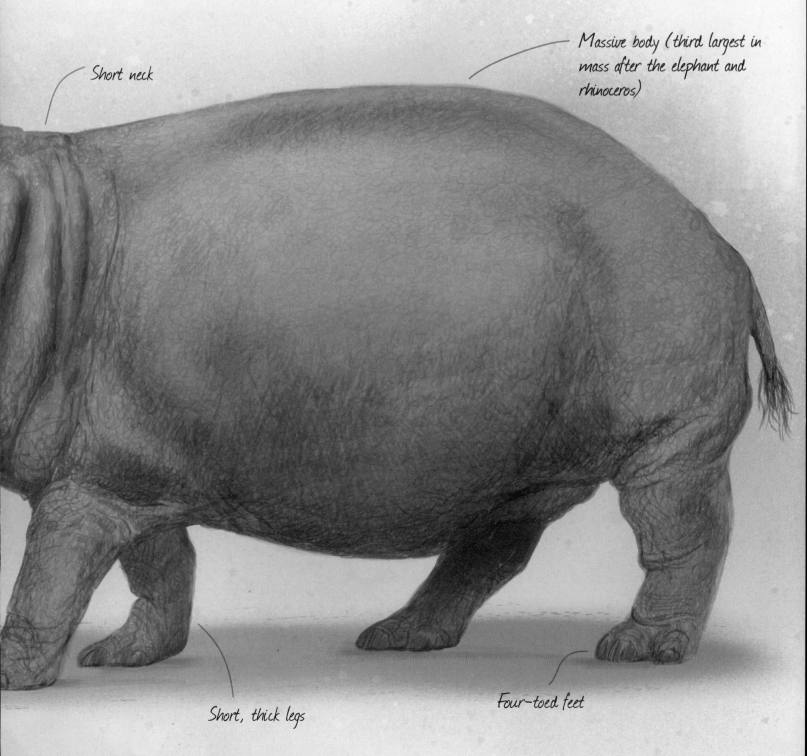

Short neck

Massive body (third largest in mass after the elephant and rhinoceros)

Short, thick legs

Four-toed feet

Giraffidae

Giraffes

The Giraffidae family is comprised of four species of giraffe and one species of okapi, all of which are found on the African continent. Unmistakable for their long necks and their unique patterns, giraffes are the tallest of all existing land mammals. They use their height to feed on the leaves of tall trees. They grasp leaves and branches with their long, bluish-purple tongues that can reach 18 inches (46 centimeters) in length. Giraffes also feed on shrubs and fruits when available. Another notable feature is their horns, called *ossicones*, which grow on both males and females from the tops of their heads. Some giraffes grow a second pair behind the primary ossicones.

Northern Giraffe

(Giraffa camelopardalis)
Found in Sudan, Ethiopia, Uganda, and Kenya, Africa. Northern Giraffes are marked with uneven brown blotches and have white legs.
Height: 17 feet (5 meters); Weight: 2,500 pounds
Conservation status: Vulnerable

Reticulated Giraffe

(Giraffa reticulata)
Predominantly found in Kenya, Africa, Reticulated Giraffes have an even, well-defined pattern marked by darker orange-brown blotches against cream-colored thin lines. They are one of the most common giraffes seen in zoos.
Height: 17 feet (5 meters)
Weight: 1,600 pounds
Conservation status: Vulnerable

Like camels, giraffes walk by moving both legs on the same side of the body at the same time

120

Masai Giraffe

(*Giraffa tippelskirchi*)
Found in Kenya and throughout Tanzania,
Africa, Masai Giraffes are the largest of all
Giraffe species. They have a darker appearance
with jagged leaf-shaped blotches and tan lines.
Height: 18 feet (5.4 meters)
Weight: 3,800 pounds
Conservation status: Vulnerable

Horns called
"ossicones" are
shorter on females
than on males

Short mane runs
the length of the
neck onto the
upper shoulder

Shapes of the
neck vertebrae
visible from
the front view

Though very long, the
giraffe's neck is made
up of 7 vertebrae,
the same number
humans have

Southern Giraffe

(*Giraffa giraffa*)
Found in South Africa, Botswana,
Namibia, Zambia, and Zimbabwe,
Southern Giraffes' patterns consist
of large, uneven notched blotches
extending to the ankles.
Height: 17 feet (5 meters)
Weight: 2,600 pounds
Conservation status: Vulnerable

Long, very thin legs

Okapis

Okapis share many of the same features with giraffes, such as their horns and long tongue. Their body size is much more suited to life in the dense undergrowth of rain forests. They have an oily coat to help keep them dry in the wet forest. Okapis are true herbivores, feeding on leaves, buds, fungi, and fruits. They occasionally eat the clay on riverbeds to supplement their diet with minerals. Solitary and territorial, okapis mark their area with a tar-like secretion from scent glands on their feet.

Okapi
(*Okapia johnstoni*)
Found in dense rain forests in the Republic of Congo, Africa, Okapias are also known as Forest Giraffes.
Length: 8 feet (2.4 meters), head and body
Weight: 770 pounds
Conservation status: Vulnerable

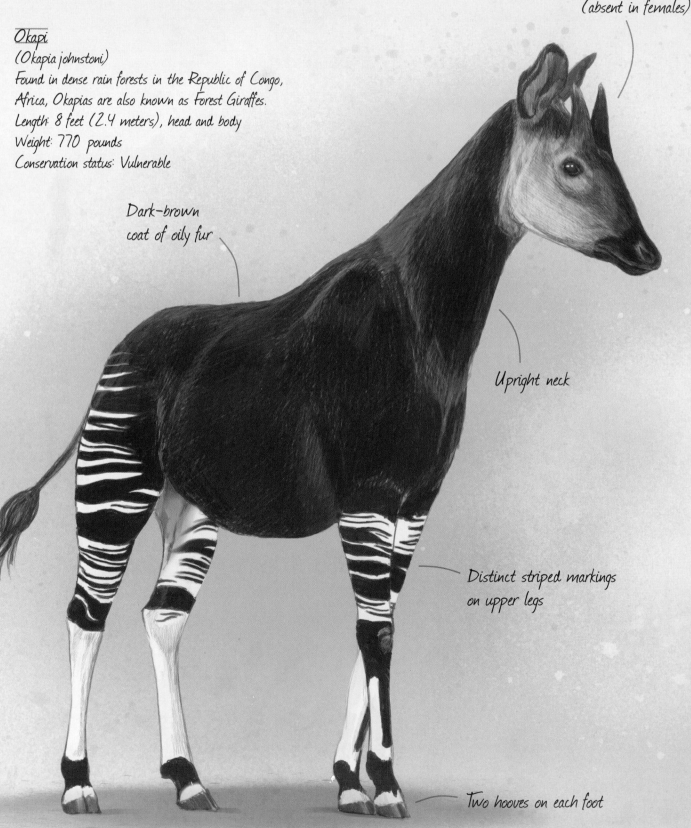

Two horns covered in skin tissue (absent in females)

Dark-brown coat of oily fur

Upright neck

Distinct striped markings on upper legs

Two hooves on each foot

Moschidae

Musk Deer

The Moschidae family is made up of seven species of musk deer, all of them from Asia and Siberia. Musk deer are small primitive deer. They lack antlers and preorbital facial scent glands found on true deer; instead musk deer secrete their musk from scent glands near their tails. (This gland is found only in males.) Males also have extended tusk-like teeth protruding from their mouths. Musk deer are solitary and eat leaves, grasses, flowers, and mosses.

Siberian Musk Deer
(Moschus moschiferus)
Found in the mountains of Northeast Asia, Siberian Musk Deer are a shy and timid species and generally solitary. Their musk is a waxy substance secreted to mark their territory and has become of great value to the perfume industry because of its potent aroma.
Length: 39 inches (1 meter), head and body
Weight: 36 pounds
Conservation status: Vulnerable

Large ears

Large, tusk-like teeth extending from mouth

Rounded ears and large, dark eyes give the Lesser Mouse-Deer its mouse-like appearance

Thin, frail legs with small hooves

Tragulidae

Chevrotains

The Tragulidae family consists of 10 species of chevrotains, also known as mouse deer due to their small size. They are the smallest of all ungulates and have very delicate frames. Chevrotains live in dense forests where their short and thin build helps them navigate tight spaces. Both male and females have tusks used for display and fighting.

Lesser Mouse-Deer
(Tragulus kanchil)
Found in Southeast Asia, Lesser Mouse-Deer are the smallest of the Tragulidae family species. They spend the daylight hours seeking shelter in thick undergrowth and move to higher ground at night to forage for fallen fruits and leaves.
Length: 18 inches (46 centimeters), head and body
Weight: 4 pounds
Conservation status: Least Concern

Cervidae

Deer

The Cervidae family is comprised of 91 species of deer, all of which have antlers (with the exception of the Chinese Water Deer). Their antlers are primarily found only on males and are shed once a year. Cervids are agile and powerful animals—some are capable of reaching speeds of 45 miles per hour (72 kilometers per hour) and leaping 30 feet (9 meters) in a single jump. They have four-chambered stomachs that require them to regurgitate and re-chew plant matter prior to digestion. This is called *rumination*, which allows them to extract nutrients from plants. Cervids are found on all continents, except Australia and Antarctica, and live in a variety of habitats, ranging from tundras to rain forests.

Reaching 53 inches (1.3 meters) in length, Reindeer have the largest antlers per body weight than any other deer species

Like other cervids, Elk antlers are covered in skin called "velvet" during their growth period

Reindeer
(Rangifer tarandus)
Found in Northern Europe, Siberia, and North America, Reindeer are the only cervids with antlers on both male and females. They are also known as Caribou in North America.
Length: 84 inches (2.1 meters), head and body
Weight: 400 pounds
Conservation status: Vulnerable

Wide hooves for footing in snow

Elk

(Cervus canadensis)
Found in North America and Central Asia, Elk live in and at the edges of forests. They feed on grasses, leaves, and plants. Males are known for having large antler displays reaching over 40 inches in length.
Length: 10 feet (3 meters), head and body
Weight: 1,000 pounds
Conservation status: Least Concern

Moose

(Alces alces)
Found in North America and across Eurasia, Moose are the largest of all cervids. They consume grasses, tree bark, and aquatic plants, eating up to 80 pounds of plant material per day. They are also known as Elk in Eurasia.
Length: 10.5 feet (3.2 meters), head and body
Weight: 1,500 pounds
Conservation status: Least Concern

Broad, flat antlers reach 83 inches (2 meters) across, and are used primarily as a display to attract mates

Large nose with small bones called "turbinates" used to warm air before it reaches the lungs

Long legs

Northern Pudú

(Pudu mephistophiles)
Found in Southern Chile and Southwestern Argentina, Northern Pudús are the smallest deer species. Their antlers grow to only 3 inches (7.6 centimeters) in length.
Length: 33 inches (84 centimeters), head and body
Weight: 26 pounds
Conservation status: Vulnerable

Bovidae

Antelopes, Cattle, and Goats

The Bovidae family is a widespread and diverse group of ungulates with over 140 species found across Africa, Asia, Europe, and North America. They include many familiar animals like goats, sheep, and cows. Like the Cervidae family (deers), bovids have four-chambered stomachs and require rumination to digest plant matter. They differ from deer in that they have no incisors or front teeth on their upper jaw. Instead bovids have a thick layer of tissue called a *dental pad*, which is used to grip grasses and plants when pressed against their lower teeth. Most bovids have single-paired horns that can be as long as 33 inches (84 centimeters), or as short as a few inches. They range in size from the 2,600 pound Asian Gaur to the minute 6-pound Royal Antelope.

Mountain Goat
(Oreamnos americanus)
Found in Western North America, Mountain Goats are expert climbers. They live on mountain sides reaching elevations of over 13,000 feet (3,962 meters). They feed on grasses, ferns, and mosses.
Length: 70 inches (1.7 meters), head and body
Weight: 300 pounds
Conservation status: Least Concern

Common Wildebeest
(Connochaetes taurinus)
Found in the Southern African continent, Common Wildebeests are also known as Blue Wildebeest or Gnus. They are large herding antelope that inhabit savanna grasslands. They feed mostly on short grasses.
Length: 94 inches (2.3 meters), head and body
Weight: 640 pounds
Conservation status: Least Concern

Long mane over neck and shoulders

Black curved horns found only on males

Large head with mane along bottom of neck

Woolly, white coat with an undercoat for protection from cold weather

Thin legs

American Bison
(Bison bison)

Found in Western North America, American Bison, also called Buffalo, are large herding animals known for their thick dense coat covering the front half of their bodies. Both powerful and athletic, the American Bison is capable of jumping 6 feet (1.8 meters) vertically and running 40 miles per hour (64 kph).
Length: 11.5 feet (3.5 meters), head and body
Weight: 2,200 pounds
Conservation status: Near Threatened

Gemsbok
(Oryx gazella)

Found in arid regions in the Southern African continent, Gemsboks live in herds of 10 to 40 individuals led by one dominant male. They graze on dry grasses and foliage.
Length: 8 feet (2.4 meters), head and body
Weight: 530 pounds
Conservation status: Least Concern

Long, slender, and sharp horns reaching 33 inches (84 centimeters) in length

Thick coat of fur covering shoulders, forelimbs, and head

Horns can reach 24 inches (61 centimeters) in length

Distinct facial markings disguise the eyes from predators

White and black markings on legs

Glossary

Arboreal: Living in trees

Carnivore: An animal that only eats the flesh of other animals

Class: A biological classification of animals or organisms that share the same common attributes. This classification falls between Phylum and Order. For the complete list of animal classification see page 4.

Crepuscular: Active primarily during twilight hours of dawn and dusk.

Diurnal: Active during the day.

Echolocation: The process of locating objects by sensing reflected echoes.

Edentate: Mammals distinguished by the lack of incisor or canine teeth (such as armadillos, anteaters, and sloths).

Family: A biological classification of animals or organisms that have similar attributes. This classification falls between Order and Genus. For the complete list of animal classification see page 4.

Folivorous: An herbivore that eats only leaves.

Fossorial: Adapted to digging and living underground.

Frugivorous: An herbivore that eats only fruits.

Genus: A biological classification of animals or organisms that share very similar attributes or are closely related. This classification falls between Family and Species. For the complete list of animal classification see page 4.

Herbivore: An animal that eats only plants and plant matter.

Kingdom: The highest rank of biological classification of living organisms. There are five Kingdoms representing all living things. For the complete list of animal classification see page 4.

Monera: One of the five kingdoms of living organisms representing single-celled organisms.

New World: Native to North, Central, and South America.

Nocturnal: Active during the night.

Old World: Native to Africa, Europe, and Asia.

Omnivore: Animals that eat both flesh and plant matter.

Order: A biological classification of animals or organisms that share attributes or traits. This classification falls between Class and Family. For the complete list of animal classification see page 4.

Phylum: A broad biological classification of animals or organisms that share attributes. This classification falls between Kingdom and Class. For the complete list of animal classification see page 4.

Prehensile: Adapted for holding and grasping, specifically a tail.

Protists: One of the five Kingdoms of living organisms representing single-celled organisms that contain a nucleus.

Rumination: A digestive process found mostly in Ungulates in which food is chewed, swallowed, then moved back to the mouth where it is chewed again prior to final digestion.

Species: The basic biological classification of animals or organisms that share the same attributes. For the complete list of animal classification see page 4.

Suborder: A biological classification of animals or organisms that share similar attributes or traits. This classification falls between Order and Family. For the complete list of animal classification see page 4.

Subspecies: The most basic biological classification of animals or organisms that share the same attributes. This is usually defined by geographical isolation. For the complete list of animal classification see page 4.

Ungulate: Mammals with hooved feet.

Vertebrae: A spinal column or any one of the individual bones that make up the spinal column.

About the Author

Juan Carlos Alonso (author and illustrator) is a Cuban American graphic designer, creative director, and illustrator. He has more than 30 years experience in the graphic design and illustration field. In 1992, he founded Alonso & Company, a creative boutique specializing in branding, design, and advertising. His passion for nature has taken him around the world from Australia to the Galapagos Islands to study animals. Along with his work in the graphic arts, he is also an accomplished wildlife sculptor focusing mostly on prehistoric animals.